Mario Sequeira has been researching on stress management in great depth much before stress was hardly heard of. He believes that when in a dark room you have two choices—curse the darkness or turn on the light. If you turn on the lights, you bring about change. He has made it his life's mission to turn on the lights for the millions in darkness.

Mario is affectionately called the Port King of Goa due to his passion for wine. He is a businessman and a prolific speaker who enjoys the company of happy thinkers. He owns and manages various resorts, wineries, hospitality and real estate businesses, and provides training and employment through his creative and design thinking programmes which are meant to teach young minds how to think creatively so as to thrive in this ever-changing world of ours. He is happily married to Jean and is the proud father of Charlene and Sheona. He is the author of the bestselling book *Killing Me Softly*.

To know more:

www.mariosequeira.org

Facebook: Mario Sequeira—Get Transformed

Insta: master.yourdestiny

Linkedin: Mario Sequeira

Praise for the Book

'The book evokes and ignites a tremendous zeal for a healthy life. It guides the reader gently by the arm as it traverses medical research, philosophical quotes and personal examples without a hint of the mundane. Great book!'

Dr Balesh Jindal,
bestselling author,
photographer, artist and
senior physician

'The book is a masterful work, an essential tool for everyone to achieve health and wellness ... it has profound wisdom yet simple to understand.'

Dr Lingaraj Nath,
writer, doctor, self-health promoter

'You wanna live long, choose wisely! There is no magic pill! Thoroughly researched and extremely informative ... this masterpiece by Mario isn't just a road map to longevity, but to good health and happiness too. A delightful must-read ... '

Dr Neuman Correia, MRCPI, MD(TCD),
endocrinologist

'This book is packed with wisdom that will help to extend your healthspan and in turn your lifespan. In my opinion, it is a must-read.'

Dr Prasanna Shah, MD, DNB,
consultant gastroenterologist,
interventional endobariatric and endoscopist,
Breach Candy Hospital Trust,
Jaslok Hospital and
Saifee Hospital

'Encounter Mario first-hand and you'll quickly recognize him as a seasoned individual, well-versed in the art of embracing life to its utmost. Within the pages of this book, he artfully intertwines his life's wisdom with meticulous research to offer you a tailored road map to a long and fulfilling existence.'

Dr Rohan Fonseca, MD,
health and lifestyle coach

'This is the book for anyone seeking to unlock the secrets to a longer, healthier and vibrant life. Written in an easy and engaging style, it is a must-read for all ages.'

Bhavna Harchandrai
celebrity fitness trainer for twenty-six years,
bestselling author, TedX speaker and
popular TV show hostess

‘Health is wealth and good health is life. This book is a perfect guide to healthier and fitter YOU, both mentally and physically.’

Savio Rodrigues
politician, author and entrepreneur

‘Filled with actionable advice, inspirational stories and thought-provoking insights, this book empowers readers to take control of their health and embrace the promise of a vibrant, fulfilling future.

Sonal Chowdhary
nutrition and medical consultant, and
bestselling author

MARIO SEQUEIRA

A ROAD MAP TO LONGEVITY

DEBUNKING MYTHS ABOUT HEALTHY LIVING

Om Books International

First published in 2024 by

Om Books International

Corporate & Editorial Office
A-12, Sector 64, Noida 201 301
Uttar Pradesh, India
Phone: +91 120 477 4100
Email: editorial@ombooks.com
Website: www.ombooksinternational.com

Sales Office
107, Ansari Road, Darya Ganj,
New Delhi 110 002, India
Phone: +91 11 4000 9000
Email: sales@ombooks.com
Website: www.ombooks.com

ISBN: 978-93-5376-849-2

Printed in India

10 9 8 7 6 5 4 3 2 1

To

Dad who taught us how to live and enjoy life

Contents

Preface

'There is only one corner of the universe that you can be certain of improving and that is your own self.'

—Aldous Huxley

What really matters to me are

- My family—I love them very dearly.
- Being able to live my life to its fullest—I am enjoying every bit of it and do not want anything to come in my way.
- To have the strength and vigour to continue having the positive impact I am having on others—the purpose of my life is to improve the lives of others.

What really matters to you?

We all know people who have died of old age. In the days gone by this was a category given when people died of unknown causes, but in the modern world it is rare not to be able to identify the cause of death making the very definition of ' death by old age' redundant.

What did the autopsy reports and medical histories of all centenarians, dying unexpectedly out of a hospital in Vienna show?[1] These autopsies were performed over a period of eighteen years. The centenarians were found to have succumbed to diseases in a 100 per cent of the cases examined. Many of them were even perceived by their physicians to be quite healthy just prior to their death. Not a single one died of old age. A majority died of cardiovascular diseases.

People die of diseases that accompany old age which are largely preventable. If you remove toxins from your body, if you learn to get the stress out of your life, if you change your environment and if you deliver nutrients to your body, you could actually reverse the biological markers of ageing. For example, you can improve your blood pressure, where possible and even your eyesight and hearing which are known to get bad with age can improve.

[1] Andrea M. Berzlanovich, Wolfgang Keil, Thomas Waldhoer, Ernst Sim, Peter Fasching, Barbara Fazeny-Dörnerhttps,'Do Centenarians Die Healthy? An Autopsy Study', National Library of Medicine, PubMed, July 2005, accessed on 28 February 2024, https://pubmed.ncbi.nlm.nih.gov/16079208

Most people think ageing is normal. But what is normal about it? There are people who are twenty-five and look forty and behave like forty while there are people at sixty who behave and have the biology of a person who is just thirty. Ageing has a genetic component but this is only partially true. If you do things that I propose with your food and lifestyle and have a healthier life you could add thirty to fifty years to your life. It is important that we not only have a long life, but also a high-quality one. Most people think that ageing is universal but there are organisms in this world, like the protozoa, the hydra and even jellyfish that almost never age.[2] Thus, there are mechanisms in Nature that can keep living beings living almost forever. We are the only species that know we age and if we consider the knowledge we now have we can use this feedback loop of information to influence and reverse the whole process of ageing. Current prevailing science wisdom says that our biological potential is 130 years though I think it is much more, but even if we take it as 130 it means that when you are sixty-five you do not even begin middle age. If you get it right, sixty-five could be the best time of your youth!

During the years it took me to write this book, I was blessed to see how these suggestions of mine practically worked. Take for example, forty-eight-year-old Pankaj Saraf whom I helped lose about 16 kg. To this day, he

---

[2] Emily Osterloff, 'Immortal Jellyfish: The Secret to Cheating Death', Natural History Museum, accessed on 19 July 2023, https://www.nhm.ac.uk/discover/immortal-jellyfish-secret-to-cheating-death.html

credits me for his fitness and is grateful that he could trek up the Himalayas because of me. Then there is David Aguiar who fondly calls me his 'deliverer of peace of mind'. Like them, many people have thanked me for improving their lives. It is because of this outpouring of gratitude that I feel encouraged to write this book.

As I researched for this book and looked into the various aspects of longevity, the world was struck by the deadly Covid-19 virus which made it even more imperative that I send out this message of hope. Have you ever asked yourself what really matters to you? Putting my suggestions into practice is not difficult. It is much like cleaning your house. No matter where you start or which room you begin with if you keep cleaning and persevere eventually the whole house becomes clean.

This is a beautiful world that you and I are a part of. Unfortunately, we only think of wealth and how to accumulate it. What we forget is that while it is important to be wealthy, it is of equal importance that we are able to enjoy the fruit of that wealth. If not, we are only earning to be able to pay our medical bills as we age.

As a kid I was neither thin nor good-looking but always aspired to be both. Due to my physique, I was regularly christened by different nicknames that were not flattering. As years went by, I continued getting larger with no clue of how to turn the situation around. By thirty-five, I had a sweet and beautiful family, a car and a house of my own and above all I was healthy. I was happy with my life and aspired to live up to 140 years. But suddenly, as if by divine intervention, I had an epiphany. I became acutely aware of my excess weight, which greatly weighed down on me. And suddenly I turned desperate to lose it.

I took to the swimming pool to do so. I would swim non-stop for an hour almost daily but to no avail. This was effortless because I enjoyed swimming. There was nothing like waking up in the morning and taking a dive into a nice warm pool of water. I would lose a kg or two in a couple of days but immediately put it all back again. Eventually, I ended up losing nothing. I was told it would help if I sped up and covered a greater distance during the hour. I swam as if chased by a shark. But I missed out on the pleasures of swimming. However, a few weeks passed and nothing happened. I simply could not lose weight since I would end up devouring anything placed in front of me after swimming. Thus, I felt healthy and happy but remained terribly out of shape. Clearly, swimming was not a solution to my obesity problem.

So a few months down the road, I joined a local health club. Going to the club was both a fascinating and an amusing experience for me. I say this in hindsight but believe me, initially it was embarrassing and intimidating. Why? You may ask. Well, Andrew the burly trainer was very welcoming and that made me feel quite comfortable. He quickly put me through a few basic exercises to gauge my abilities and shortcomings. In a few moments, he got me to lie down on a floor mat where I was to do a few abdominal exercises. As I lay on the mat, I had a sinking feeling. (Getting onto the mat was quite a feat as I could not bend down easily. I was after all more than 117 kg.) Anyway, I was promptly surrounded by five cheering young studs. These guys with six-packs were shouting, 'Come on, you can do it', in unison. In the background, I could hear the trainer call out, 'One, two, three', encouraging me to do the abdominals. Given my poor fitness, I just could not go beyond the count of three! I was stuck. My body and mind were tearing apart. Since I could not go further, Andrew stopped counting and the hurrahs went silent.

Anyway, I did not give up easily and eventually over a period of time could do about forty crunches without too much ado. *I felt good but still did not lose weight*. It just was not happening. I was trying but nothing was working.

With time, I became an avid treadmill user but I would lose weight for a few days only. What was worse was that I not only put it all back, but also added a little more to it. A long-term solution to weight loss evaded me.

Was it because losing weight needed to be looked into more holistically? Could it be that I had to look at health rather than just weight loss? Could it be because it had to be a combination of weights, aerobics and a diet plan? Or was it all this and more?

It felt terrible. I had all the wealth I needed to have a good life but I would rather have died than be forced into a diet plan that would almost starve me to death. Doing weights and aerobics could be fun but following a proper diet would be a challenge. It was pretty much apparent to me that none of what I was doing was of much help. By now I knew that focusing a lot on my abdomen and related exercise was not the right thing to do. It had to be a combination of exercise, a reasonable diet plan and much more. What about my overall health? If I was serious and really aspired to live to a healthy and happy 140, I needed a plan. I was preparing myself for the long haul but on the following non-negotiable terms. I refused to change my social life or my eating habits by a yard but I knew that I would have to tweak it all. Rules were never meant for me and I was not just about to put myself under the command of some dietician or yoga guru. I knew I would never be able to sustain that unless (just like when I gave up smoking) I studied life in detail, understood the paradigm, convinced myself of the way forward and got going.

I have studied and researched until I finally have developed a road map to a long healthy and happy life. The road is not difficult. All it takes is a vision and years of consistency and perseverance. Be the master of your destiny. I do not promise to make you a superhuman but I assure you that after you read this book, you will realize that being human is super.

There is a real possibility that after reading this book your life will never be the same again, so brace yourself and prepare to embrace all the good that awaits you!

After years of trials and errors, I now have in my possession the secrets to weight loss and a road map to a long and healthy life. I would like to share these with you. After reading this book, I am sure you will be excited to embark on a journey of developing a happy, healthy, long and delightful life.

If you follow what I have written in this book, your quality of life will improve drastically. You will be fitter to fight many more pandemics to follow and the longevity of your life will increase greatly.

I hope to challenge your present paradigms and give you food for thought on the new possibilities of good health and happiness that you could enjoy should you decide to tweak the way you think.

The Blueprint for a Healthy, Happy and Long Life

1

'It isn't the mountains ahead to climb that wear you out; it's the pebble in your shoe.'

Muhammad Ali

Why Is Life So Unpredictable?

Antonio was a wise old man who had lived an unconventional but a healthy life. He was often found puffing away at his white, clay pipe which had darkened and with use had actually turned ebony. At times, he would enjoy a Scotch, beer or wine, in enviable quantities. Spicy crabs and clams to rare meats and vegetables kept the epicure hale and hearty.

Antonio enjoyed the company of family and friends in equal measure. He was the very soul of our family. He was not only in good shape physically and mentally, but also ready to party till the cows came home. It looked as if he was set to live heartily and healthily for many more years. I was expecting him to cross 120. But to my utter dismay, towards the end of 2002, my hale and hearty ninety-two-year-old father, Antonio Sequeira, was diagnosed with liver cancer. Suddenly, his health spiralled out of control much like an F-16 fighter jet whose guidance systems had shut down making it hurtle earthwards leaving no time for its pilot to eject. He passed away just a few months later.

Dad was enjoying his life and we were thoroughly enjoying seeing him grow old. Unlike many cantankerous nonagenarians, this ninety-two-year-old was happy to live life to the fullest and shared his joy with all who came his way. He had the money and his family to back him. He had it all and yet away he left us abruptly ...

It was during those difficult days that I asked myself, *Was there anything that my father could have done to prolong his life?*

He was happy, wealthy and even blessed with good health. He had the money to spend on medical support but beyond a point even the best of doctors could not save him. I demanded answers!

‘Are you earning today only to be able to pay your medical bills at a later date?’

And it soon became obvious to me that money although important cannot buy you good health and happiness.

Are you earning today only to be able to pay your medical bills at a later date?

Understanding Ageing

In my quest for answers, I read about an incident that occurred more than a century ago.

Armed with the latest technology of their times, the Inuit hunters were sure their prey was within grasp. (You may know them as Eskimos, but the people of the Arctic are officially called the Inuit.) They fired a lance bomb filled with the all-powerful gunpowder and were sure it had hit their prey. The design was such that upon impact it would easily pierce the thick blubber of a bowhead whale. The lance was fired, but they struggled to rein in their prize much to their dismay and thus missed out on a tasty and a super-nourishing meal.

This was in 1887.

The whale escaped only to be caught 120 years later when another group of Inuit hunters finally trapped it. They found fragments of the original lance still embedded in its blubber.[3]

It is estimated that these whales generally live for at least 150 years and at times more than 210. I find it astonishing that the bowhead whale not only survived the hit without any medical help, but also managed to live an

[3] Erin Conroy, 'Netted Whale Hit by Lance a Century Ago', Science News, 13 June 2007, accessed on 22 June 2023, https://www.nbcnews.com/id/wbna19195624

additional 120 years. Ageing is a mystery we know very little about, yet it comes without much effort. If we could slow it just a little bit, the benefits to humanity would be phenomenal. A majority of chronic human diseases have their roots in the ageing process but biomedical science is majorly focused on managing diseases like diabetes, cardiovascular disease (CVD), cancer and Alzheimer's.

By delaying ageing, we could delay the onset of most of these diseases which come with age.[4]

How Medicines Have Failed Us

I profoundly respect doctors and the entire medical world for their enormous contributions to the well-being of humanity but if improving the health of their patients was their goal in the past few decades, they have taken their eyes off the ball. With so many 'anti' medicines like antibiotics, antidepressants, antihistamines in the market, they seem to have missed out on the pro-health factors like vitamins, tonics, exposing oneself to the morning sun or even focussing on stress management, which till the last few decades were the foundations of medicine.

---

[4] Elin Martine Doeland, 'Can We Slow Down Ageing', Institute of Clinical Medicine, University of Oslo, 2 December 2022, accessed on 27 June 2023, https://www.med.uio.no/klinmed/english/research/news-and-events/news/2022/can-we-slow-down-ageing.html

Medicine has become a science of treating symptoms rather than healing the root cause of the symptoms. It appears that the entire medical industry is geared to treat sickness rather than to prevent it. There is however no doubt that in many ways it has contributed to the increased longevity of life. Through all this, one lingering thought comes to my mind, *Could we have done better*?

The objective of this book is neither to denigrate wealth which is critical for our survival and comfort, nor undermine medicine or doctors who are equally important for our existence. But to remind you that it is high time we place a 'price tag' on our health. We must look at health as a major asset that needs to be managed just like our asset portfolio. It needs to be nurtured so that it sustains us for long.

Your body has a self-repairing system[5] which should ensure that you wake up refreshed in the morning. If you are not waking up that way, it is because you are not giving your body enough or the right repair material it requires for maintenance work. To make matters worse, you add to its toxic load which interferes with its functioning and confuses signalling between cells. You age because of the cumulative repair deficits of each of these nights when your body cannot heal itself because you do not supply

---

[5] Kuei-Hui Chu, Heng-Hsin Tung, Daniel L. Clinciu, Hua-I Hsu, Yi-Chen Wu, Ching-I Hsu, Shu-Wei Lin, Shi-Jun Pan, 'Gerontology and Geriatric Medicine', PubMed Central, National Library of Medicine, 24 March 2022, accessed on 27 June 2023, https://www.ncbi.nlm.nih.gov/pmc/articles/PMC8958667/#:~:text=The%20human%20body%20has%20tremendous,to%20heal%20and%20recover%20physically.

the repair materials while simultaneously confusing it with toxins that it cannot handle.[6]

Having been a student of chemistry, I have been reading and studying research papers to understand longevity. I decided to leave the complexities of modern medicine to doctors and studied the basic chemistry of health and its management. Much like Sherlock Holmes, I picked up a magnifying glass and set off to unearth the hidden mysteries of life. I have since shovelled out buried secrets that humanity had lost many decades ago.

Most of us try to reverse ageing to look better. We seek to pick up creams that will magically do away with our wrinkles and make us look much younger. As Andy Rooney, the American writer, producer and humourist puts it, 'It's paradoxical that the idea of living a long life appeals to everyone, but the idea of getting old doesn't appeal to anyone.'

Looks make a difference, but we must work on an inside-out approach rather than the reverse.

Understanding Your Body

Even though medicine has got complex, physically the human body has barely changed over the past thousands of years.[7] We are all made from one cell. Indeed it would

---

[6] Thomas Johnson, Jenna Fletcher, 'Why Sleep Is Essential for Health', Medical NewsToday, 6 January 2023, accessed on 27 June 2023, https://www.medicalnewstoday.com/articles/325353

[7] Alan R. Templeton, 'Has Human Evolution Stopped?', PubMed

not be wrong for me to say, 'In the beginning there was a cell.' A human body is actually a conglomeration of trillions of cells. If we could find a way of keeping the unit we call 'the cell' healthy, it would solve a majority of our health issues. This is not a figment of my imagination. Studies have shown that all cells are inherently the same and that stem cells can be picked up from any part of our body and made to develop completely differently when placed in a different environment.[8] While studying the body from this angle, I am convinced that if we could keep our cells in a state of homeostasis we could have a much longer, healthier and happier life. [9]

There are two factors that greatly affect the normal functions of cells. One of these works for the cell's well-being while the other has the potential of destroying them. The first one being nutrients (vitamins, carbohydrates, proteins, fat, minerals, etc.) and the second being toxins like nicotine, impure air, pesticides in food, etc. The toxins that you gladly put into your body, unknown to you, poison your cells.

Central, National Library of Medicine, 2 July 2010, accessed on 27 June 2023, https://www.ncbi.nlm.nih.gov/pmc/articles/PMC3721656

8 James McIntosh, 'What Are Stem Cells, and What Do They Do?', Medical NewsToday, 19 October 2018, accessed on 24 May 2023, https://www.medicalnewstoday.com/articles/323343

9 A Cleveland Medical Professional, 'Stem Cells', Cleveland Clinic, Reviewed on 22 March 2023, accessed on 18 June 2023, https://my.clevelandclinic.org/health/body/24892

Your life is yours only once and your body is the only one you will ever have. Give it a chance to live well and it will show you, life, as you have never before imagined. The fascinating thing is that *it is incredibly easy to live a wonderful healthy and long life*. It is not cumbersome at all. A magical combination of wealth and good health will help you enjoy the various seasons of life in all their splendour and glory. Many of us miss out on these not because we do not seek but only because we look in the wrong direction. Spending too much time in the gym or at work, may be good but you do not need to waste so much time on these activities.

The Great Architect of the Universe has not spared any effort to make living easy and comfortable for us. Medicines should be the last recourse. Unfortunately, we use them as the first, only because we are lazy and refuse to understand the fundamentals of life or our body.

We send a spacecraft to Mars and know the precise moment and point at which it will land. We know this to the second. We check our weather apps and know if it will rain or snow tomorrow. We even know the exact time when the sun will rise a thousand years from today, yet we do not trust our body which is another marvellous creation by the Creator of our perfect universe. We do not appreciate its ability to take care of itself and so do not bother to give it the materials required for it to carry out its own repair work. Sadly, our bodies do not come with a user manual but I am convinced that we are all wired to live more than a healthy 140 years!

As the former football coach, Marv Levy, puts it: 'Age is inevitable. Ageing isn't.'

I am confident that if you follow everything I have written in this book you will be able to improve the quality of your life drastically. You will be fitter to fight many pandemics and your longevity of life will increase by anywhere from 30–40 per cent of what it would have normally been.

What Ails the World's Oldest Supercomputer?

2

'One of the biggest lies in the story of humanity is the lie of our imperfection.'

Miguel Angel Ruiz

We belong to an amazing world. Human beings are God's greatest creation. Our body is truly perfect.

Human Body: The Oldest Supercomputer

The human body is a dynamic framework of bones and cartilages, which is firm and interwoven with hinges and joints. In many cases, the joints are seamless making body movements possible and painless. Hidden from sight it has a lubricating machine cushioning the body from pain that would have been caused by friction of moving parts. The lubricant also reduces joint wear and tear.[10] Think of how sophisticated this is. All machines known to me need to be lubricated externally but the human body has it all preset and to precision. This supercomputer also runs an inbuilt chemical factory that is more intricate than ever imaginable. It transforms the food we eat into energy and living tissue. It delivers chemicals which assist repairs when cells are damaged due to accident or overwork. The energy produced empowers us to enjoy the world around us and enables us to work and play. Our body has a cooling and heating system which keeps us from freezing in cold temperatures and burning in the heat. This inbuilt thermostat never fails. If it gets too hot, drops of sweat pour out of our skin to cool us down.[11] The brain is the Central Processing Unit of this supercomputer. It controls every action from the quiver of a finger to the movements of our eyelids.

While in machines and man-made computers information and signals are carried across by wires and cables, our body carries them through nerves and blood vessels. These human cables carry current, information

---

10 Helmut Tributsch, *How Life Learned to Live: Adaptation in Nature*, The MIT Press, 1984.

11 Alex Brashears, 'Hypothalamus', Ask A Biologist, Arizona State University School of Life Sciences, 9 June 2012, accessed on 28 June 2023, https://askabiologist.asu.edu/bird-hypothalamus

and guidance to the various organs of our body making it possible for our eyes to synchronize with our feet and our mouths to speak what our mind thinks. It enables us to dream and take action to make them come true.

Our eyes are an awesome camera which scan the world and save pictures to its memory without a limit, without even the click of a button.

Our body without doubt is an engineering marvel, but do we ever take a moment to understand how intricate and special it is? Our brain performs ten quadrillion operations per second without us ever knowing.[12] What is making blood flow through our body at the right pace? What makes the heart beat for a lifetime? How do the many trillion cells synchronize every second?

Dr George McGavin, one of the UK's foremost entomologists and leading authorities on the natural world, a respected academic, author, television and radio presenter describes human limbs as a triumph of complex engineering. He explains how the hand not only gives a solid grip, but also manipulates small objects with great precision. The versatility of our hands sets us apart from every other living creature

---

[12] Charles Q. Choi, '"Artificial Synapses" Could Let Supercomputers Mimic the Human Brain', Scientific American, 20 June 2016, accessed on 24 May 2023, https://www.scientificamerican.com/article/artificial-synapses-could-let-supercomputers-mimic-the-human-brain/

[13] George McGavin, 'The incredible human hand and foot', BBC, 18 February 2014, accessed on 18 June 2023, https://www.bbc.com/news/science-environment-26224631

on this planet. Most of its movements are controlled by muscles that are not even located in it, but are in the forearm. The muscles of the forearm connect to the finger bones via long tendons that pass through a flexible wrist. This remote musculature gives the fingers movement and phenomenal strength that would not be practicable if all muscles had to be attached directly to the wrist. In effect, the hand is simply a bony puppet, lashed together by ligaments and controlled by the forearm. It is because of this intricate network that the hand can do so much. At one extreme is the impressive strength in a climber's hand. Through habitual use and training even a single finger can support their entire body weight. At the other extreme is a concert pianist who needs great finesse which comes from intrinsic muscles in the hand.

How do we know if something is smooth or rough, wet or dry, hot or cold?

Our skin is very specialized. There are four main skin receptors that respond to light and deep pressure, touch, pain and temperature.

What about proprioception?[14] It is the sense that tells us where the various parts of our body are in space. Even with our eyes shut we can touch our nose. Sense organs in our muscles and joints tell the brain exactly when our limbs move and precisely how tense our muscles need

14 J.L. Taylor, 'Proprioception', Science Direct, 5 Nov 2008, accessed on 28 June 2023, https://www.sciencedirect.com/science/article/abs/pii/B9780080450469019070

to be to complete a given activity. It is this continuous feedback system between muscle and brain that detects minute changes that allows us to balance.

The hand might seem to be the most interesting bit of our anatomy but the foot is equally complex.[15]

Containing twenty-six bones, thirty-three joints, nineteen muscles and fifty-seven ligaments, it is one of the few pieces of anatomy that can compete with the hand for sheer complexity. Our feet need to be strong enough to deal with some of the greatest forces experienced by the body, whilst also being capable of movements as exquisite as a ballerina's pirouette. In many ways, it is because of the foot that we have evolved such extraordinary hands. The ability to walk upright meant early humans could not only cover great distances efficiently, but also use their hands to develop their unique anatomy and capabilities.

At the core of the foot is the arch. The metacarpals create space for a tough web of muscles and ligaments that play a vital role. They absorb the pressure created when we walk or run. The arch also acts as a spring, storing and releasing energy when we push off with our toes. Standing still may seem a simple act, but it is not. There is a lot happening just to keep us upright.

'The human body houses within it the most sophisticated computer ever built.'

Our body is a biomechanical marvel which has helped us master

[15] Dr George McGavin 'The Incredible Human Hand and Foot', BBC News Science, 18 February 2014, accessed on 28 June 2023, https://www.bbc.com/news/science-environment-26224631

the natural world. The human body houses within it the most sophisticated computer ever built.

Don't you think you have to find a way of taking care of this marvel before it self-destructs?

Isn't it great to be human?

Shouldn't we feel blessed to have such a perfect body?

You are a masterpiece.

As Daniela Ismerio puts it, 'The human body is simply the most beautiful complexity.'

This Thing Called Longevity Exists Out There

We have it within us to live a long, healthy and happy life way beyond a hundred years. The key lies in us.

'Human lifespan has been increasing over recent decades and is expected to swell again after a setback caused by the pandemic, with one scientist predicting that a man born in 1970 could live until 141, and females, up to a maximum of 131 years old.' [16]

Then we have the Hunzas. Some refer to them as the happiest and healthiest people on this planet. This Himalayan tribe is known for their high life expectancy.

The average life expectancy of the Hunza people is said to be 100 years, while many even exceed 120. This, notably, has been a mystery for several scientists and doctors in the world.

---

[16] Editor's Pick, 'Men Could Live to 140 as Human Lifespan Increases, Say Scientists', Juta Medical Brief, accessed on 24 May 2023, https://www.medicalbrief.co.za/men-could-live-to-140-as-human-lifespan-increases-say-scientists

One such scientist was Dr Robert MacCrison who lived with the tribe for several years. Strangely, he could not come across a single person suffering from cancer, stomach ulcers, appendicitis or any other disease.[17]

Dr Henry Coanda is another scientist who lived with them and carried deep research into their lifestyle and wrote a book where he described several reasons for the longevity of the tribe.

The life expectancy of the Hunza inhabitants was also the subject of James Hilton's novel *Lost Horizon*, which was later made into a film by Frank Capra by the same name. The book talks about a secret kingdom high in the mountains, away from the world.

All the researchers who lived with the Hunza tribe and studied them deduced that the long and healthy life of the Hunzas is because of their 'organic and natural lifestyle'. It is pertinent to note that the diet of Hunza people mainly constitutes organic raw vegetables and fruits with low protein content. Water is also one of the key factors that lead to their longevity.

In addition to their diet, their hard work also plays a key role in keeping them healthy.

---

[17] Zee Media Bureau, 'Happiest & Healthiest People on This Planet, Curious Case of Hunza Tribe!' Zeenews.India.com, accessed on 30 November 2023, https://zeenews.india.com/photos/world/happiest-healthiest-people-on-this-planet-curious-case-of-hunza-tribe-2357101

Imagine what life would be if we could live with a combination of great wealth and super health? We will not die at the age of sixty-five or even eighty-five.

Then we have the blue zones where people live very long and happy lives. What began as a National Geographic expedition, led by Dan Buettner, to uncover the secrets of longevity, evolved into the discovery of the five places around the world—Okinawa, Japan; Sardinia, Italy; Nicoya, Costa Rica; Ikaria, Greece; and Loma Linda, California—where people consistently live over 100 years old, dubbed the Blue Zones.[18] These people live lives without prescription drugs and medical appointments. In the Okinawa Blue Zone, they boast about having more than a thousand healthy, active and happy centenarians.

The Okinawa Centenarian Study,[19] started by Dr Makoto Suzuki back in 1975, is the world's longest, continuously running study of centenarians. The team has studied more than a thousand centenarians and to understand the genetic and environmental lifestyle factors responsible for healthy ageing. Here, Dr Willcox explains some of the secrets to living a long and healthy life, the Okinawan way, which really boils down to 'balance'.

---

[18] Dan Buettner and Sam Skemp, 'Blue Zones: Lessons From the World's Longest Lived', *American Journal of Lifestyle Medicine*, July 2016, accessed on 24 May 2023, https://www.ncbi.nlm.nih.gov/pmc/articles/PMC6125071/#section2-1559827616637066title

[19] Makoto Suzuki, 'The Okinawa Centenarian Study 1975', accessed on 29 June 2023 https://orcls.org/ocs

- Eat healthy and exercise.
- Be positive and find your *ikigai*—a sense of purpose in life.
- Stay mentally engaged.
- Join a *moai*, a social group.
- Stress less and rethink your relationship with time.
- Embrace your spirituality.[20]

Throughout the centuries, there have been thousands of failed theories about diet and diseases. Disease was supposed to be caused by evil spirits, then we had astrologers who would tell us that we were helpless and controlled by our star signs and the planets that ruled us. Then there was the fat theory that shamed fats (now they say it is not that bad after all). We pushed fat off our table but still got fatter.

Epigenetics exposes us to the mind-boggling idea that we have it within us to live to 140 years or even more. We just need to create the right environment for our cells to get us there. We have been brought up expecting medicine to deliver a magic pill to enhance our lifespan but we are absolutely wrong. There is no magic pill and there is none on its way. It does not even make economic sense for the pharma industry to provide us with one. The magic is within us. *It is within you*. Learn to tap into it. While medicine and pharmaceutical companies have done a

[20] Kate Whiting, 'Want to Live a Long, Healthy Life? 6 Secrets from Japan's Oldest People', World Economic Forum, 29 September 2021, accessed on 24 May 2023, https://www.weforum.org/agenda/2021/09/japan-okinawa-secret-to-longevity-good-health/

great job in the past few decades, in many ways they have got so commercialized that many in the industry have a vested interest in seeing that the sick continue being sick and the healthy also join the not-so-well category so that the multitude of unwell remains ever increasing.

In India, studies among doctors in Kerala found that even though the life expectancy of the Kerala populace was 74.9 years, the mean age of death of a Keralite doctor as per the Indian Medical Association was 61.75 years.[21] Isn't this really tragic? Doctors are expected to be the wise ones knowing the secrets of life, but could it be that longevity of life has more to it than just medicine?

We seek advice from doctors on what we should do for health and longevity. If they are the keepers of all knowledge regarding longevity, shouldn't they be living way beyond the average lifespan and not far below it?

Disease and Data

In many ways, *we become what we eat*. What we are today is based on what we have eaten over the past many years. The World Health Organization (WHO) claimed that the inadequate intake of three critical micronutrients zinc, vitamin A and iron was responsible for a number of

[21] Indian Medical Association research study, 'Kerala Doctors Die Earlier than General Public', India Times, 20 November 2017, accessed on 29 June 2023, https://timesofindia.indiatimes.com/city/kochi/docs-die-early-than-gen-public-study/articleshow/61716443.cms

sicknesses.[22] There are about ninety essential nutrients but they prioritized these three given their benefits. When deficient, they cause the most damage. The six essential nutrients are vitamins, minerals, protein, fats, water and carbohydrates which people need to consume from dietary sources for proper body function. [23]There are two reasons that these are called essential nutrients. Firstly, we must consume them either as food or as supplements because our body cannot make them, secondly because their absence could result in us getting sick. Essential nutrients are divided into two categories: micronutrients and macronutrients. Micronutrients are nutrients that a person needs in small doses. These include vitamins and minerals. Although the body only needs small amounts of them, a deficiency can cause ill health. In my opinion, the odds of getting all essential minerals through our food are zilch.

A 2020 WHO report states that the global spending on health continually rose between 2000 and 2018 and reached US $8.3 trillion or 10 per cent of the global GDP.[24] In 2021, health spending per person in the US was

---

[22] World Health Organization, 'Micronutrient Impact', Health topics, accessed on 29 June 2023, https://www.who.int/health-topics/micronutrients#tab

[23] Jenna Fletcher, Medically reviewed by Miho Hatanaka, 'What Are the 6 Essential Nutrients?', MedicalNewsToday, 22 August 2019, accessed on 29 June 2023, https://www.medicalnewstoday.com/articles/326132

[24] World Health Organization, 'Global Spending on Health: Weathering the Storm', 10 December 2020, accessed on 24 May

$12,914, which was $5,000 more than any other high-income nation.[25]

Guess where the highest-spending country was ranked out of fifty in terms of life expectancy in 2020? The US which spent $10,921 per capita was ranked 47th behind Thailand which spent only $296 per capita at 46th and just ahead of Seychelles which was 48th and spent $840 per capita. Japan which spent less than half the amount spent by the US, ranked first.[26]

There Is More to Longevity Than Just Medicine

Why is it that the country which spent the most on health was not the one with the highest life expectancy? Why was it not even among the top 5 or even top 10?

Coming to our very own India, Delhi has the highest life expectancy at birth but the Andaman and Nicobar

---

2023, https://www.who.int/publications/i/item/9789240017788

[25] Matthew McGough, Imani Telesford, Shameek Rakshit, Emma Wager, Krutika Amin and Cynthia Cox, 'How Does Health Spending in the US Compare to Other Countries?' Peterson-KFF Health System Tracker, 9 February 2023, accessed on 24 May 2023, https://www.healthsystemtracker.org/chart-collection/health-spending-u-s-compare-countries/#GDP%20per%20capita%20and%20health%20consumption%20spending%20per%20capita,%202021%20(U.S.%20dollars,%20PPP%20adjusted)

[26] Truman Du, 'Charted: Healthcare Spending and Life Expectancy, by Country', HealthCare, 13 November 2022, accessed on 29 June 2023, https://www.visualcapitalist.com/cp/healthcare-spending-versus-life-expectancy-by-country

Islands ranks second in life expectancy at birth even though their health facilities are not a shadow of those to be found in Delhi.[27]

During the past forty years, obesity in the West has grown into an epidemic. While in India due to environmental and lifestyle changes caused by industrialization, migration to urban areas, rising per capita spending and a culture of eating out, obesity has really taken off. Over the last fifteen years, it has almost reached epidemic proportions. In 2021, about 6.4 per cent of women and 4.0 per cent of men aged 15–49 were obese. Approximately 17.6 per cent women and 18.9 per cent men in the same age group are overweight, but not yet obese. This means that about a fourth of young women in India are overweight and a little over a fifth of men are above the normal body weight.[28]

Worldwide diabetes has increased manifold and has also taken on overwhelming proportions. The number of people with diabetes rose from 108 million in 1980 to 422 million in 2014. This deadly disease was estimated to be effecting 463 million in 2019 and the number is

---

27 List_of_Indian_states_by_life_expectancy_at_birth', Human Development Index Report, United Nations Development Programme , India, 2019, accessed on 18 June 2023, https://en.wikipedia.org/wiki/List_of_Indian_states_by_life_expectancy_at_birth

28 Nikhil Rampal, 'Indians Are Growing Fatter, And the Problem is Biggest for Wealthy Women, Shows NFHS Data', The Print, 5 February 2023, accessed on 1 Jul 2023, https://theprint.in/health/indians-are-growing-fatter-and-the-problem-is-biggest-for-wealthy-women-shows-nfhs-data/1350501

projected to reach about seven hundred million by 2045. Shockingly, one in two people living with diabetes do not know that they have the disease.[29] Prevalence has been rising more rapidly in low and middle-income countries than in high-income countries. In 2019, diabetes and kidney disease due to diabetes caused an estimated two million deaths.[30]

India's tryst with diabetes takes it on a very similar trajectory as it is an obesity epidemic. Did you know that more than 80–90 per cent diabetics are obese?[31]With obesity and diabetes come more than a handful of other chronic ailments like cardiovascular disease, gall bladder disease, Alzheimer's, asthma, fatty liver disease,

---

29 Pouya Saeedi, Inga Petersohn, Paraskevi Salpea, Belma Malanda, Suvi Karuranga, Nigel Unwin, Stephen Colagiuri, Leonor Guariguata, Ayesha A. Motala, Katherine Ogurtsova, Jonathan E. Shaw, Dominic Bright and Rhys Williams, 'Global and Regional Diabetes Prevalence Estimates for 2019 and Projections for 2030 and 2045: Results from the International Diabetes Federation Diabetes Atlas, 9th edition', PubMed Central, National Library of Medicine, 10 September 2019, accessed on 29 June 2023, https://pubmed.ncbi.nlm.nih.gov/31518657

30 World Health Organization, 'Diabetes', 5 April 2023, accessed on 24 May 2023, https://www.who.int/news-room/fact-sheets/detail/diabetes

31 Roch A. Nianogo, Onyebuchi A. Arah 'Forecasting Obesity and Type 2 Diabetes Incidence and Burden: The ViLA-Obesity Simulation Model', Frontiers in Public Health, 5 April 2022, accessed on 1 July 2023, https://www.frontiersin.org/articles/10.3389/fpubh.2022.818816/full#:~:text=Almost%2080%E2%80%9390%25%20of%20type,patients%20are%20overweight%20or%20obese

osteoarthritis, cancer. One feeds off the other. As one gets fatter, the risk of diabetes and all the other related sicknesses increases sharply, which greatly affects the quality of life. Even the risk of early death increases dramatically.

Whatever makes us fat also makes us sick. What makes us obese and what makes us diabetics?[32]

Obesity-related Diseases

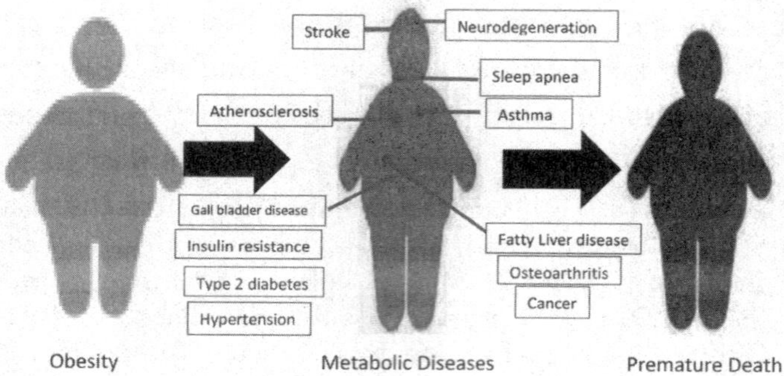

Source: International Diabetes Federation, *India Diabetes Report 2000 to 2045*, IDF Diabetes Atlas, 10th Edition, 2021, accessed on 30 June 2023, https://diabetesatlas.org/data/en/country/93/in.html

Could it be that medicine as we know it today has missed out something crucial and so has not been able to do away with diabetes?

Could it be that we need to look elsewhere for a solution to diabetes?

---

[32] Gary Taubes, *Why We Get Fat—What To Do About It*, Knopf Doubleday Publishing Group, 2011.

When AIDS was rampant, preventive programmes were organized to build awareness of its dangers and ways to avoid it. They educated citizens on the ways to avoid contracting the disease altogether and soon we saw the AIDS curve drop sharply. The same was true when the medical community went after tuberculosis. One could see an escalation and then soon after that a sharp decline. Why have we not done this for obesity or diabetes? Could it be because diabetes does not kill immediately? Could some in the health industry see diabetes as a convenient ailment that will keep churning out patients to be treated for various ailments thus keeping the cash machine ringing? Or could it be that the medical fraternity have taken their eyes off this ball because it is not life threatening?

Let me share a popular Native American parable which sums up our tryst with health.

An old Cherokee is teaching his grandson about life.

'A fight is going on inside me,' he said to the boy. 'It is a terrible fight and it is between two wolves. One is evil—he is anger, envy, sorrow, regret, greed, arrogance, self-pity, guilt, resentment, inferiority, lies, false pride, superiority and ego.'

He continued, 'The other is good—he is joy, peace, love, hope, serenity, humility, kindness, benevolence, empathy, generosity, truth, compassion and faith. The same fight is going on inside you—and inside every other person too.'

The grandson thought about it for a minute and then asked his grandfather, 'Which wolf will win?'

The old Cherokee replied, 'The one you feed.'

We get to make the choice that will determine the quality of our life both in the short as well as in the long run.

What Ails Man?

'Life is not a problem to be solved but a reality to be experienced.'—Soren Kierkegaard

It is vital to understand the various avoidable causes of death. We have been made to think that with age it is normal to lose one's memory and other motor skills. We believe it is a part of the ageing process. Recent studies however show that it is not true. Ageing is about the clock of life ticking but senescence is about how the body degrades as we grow older.[33] It is senescence that we need to take care of. Age will take care of itself.

I would encourage you to avoid 'quick-fix medical solutions'. Always try to find out the root cause of a problem. When there is a problem with an overflowing wash basin, it makes sense to turn off the faucet first and then mop the floor else the basin will keep overflowing. Many diabetic patients can get off their pills[34] if only they

---

[33] Bennett G. Childs, Matej Durik, Darren J. Baker and Jan M. van Deursen, 'Cellular Senescence in Ageing and Age-related Disease: From Mechanisms to Therapy', National Library of Medicine, PubMed Central, 10 February 2016, accessed on 23 July 2023, https://www.ncbi.nlm.nih.gov/pmc/articles/PMC4748967

[34] Mary West, Medically reviewed by Kelly Wood, 'Is Type 2 Diabetes Reversible?', Medical NewsToday, 27 August 2021, accessed on 23 July 2023,https://www.medicalnewstoday.com/articles/type-2-diabetes-reversible

follow a proper lifestyle regimen but instead of 'turning off the faucet' most just go on having pills.

You must take charge of your life. It is yours and you are the only one responsible for it. *A doctor may advise you but you have to take responsibility for your own health.*

People with Diabetes in India (in 1,000s)

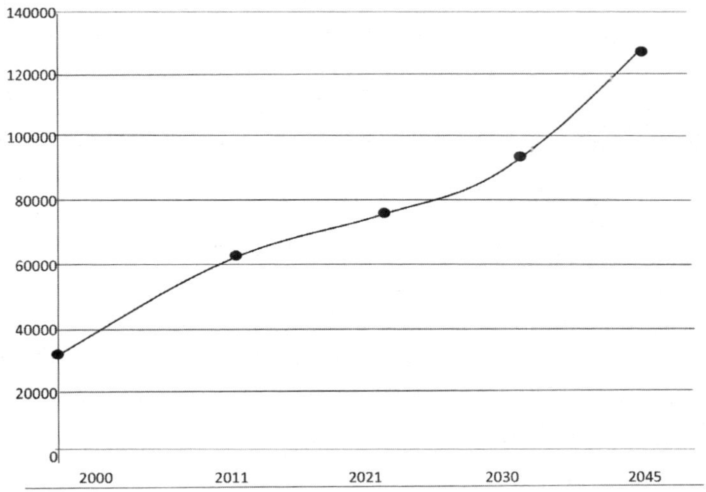

Source: International Diabetes Federation, India Diabetes Report 2000 to 2045, IDF Diabetes Atlas, 10th Edition, 2021, accessed on 30 June 2023, https://diabetesatlas.org/data/en/country/93/in.html

Ischemic heart disease, stroke and diabetes are the major causes of death worldwide. A majority of people who died from Covid-19 also suffered from diabetes, heart disease and hypertension.[35]

The Centers for Disease Control and Prevention clearly states that if we expose ourselves too much to the following factors, it would greatly increase the risk of coronary artery disease (CAD) or coronary heart disease or ischemic heart disease:

- Uncontrolled diabetes
- Obesity
- High cholesterol
- High blood pressure
- Too much stress
- Smoking, and
- Too much of junk food[36]

If the reverse is true and that by reducing any of the above we improve our heart health would I not be right to infer that heart disease is caused by all the above factors and by controlling diabetes, losing weight, lowering cholesterol, managing stress (thereby keeping blood pressure under control) not smoking and avoiding junk food we could reduce heart disease and live longer and healthier lives?

---

35 WHO, 'The Top 10 Causes of Death', 9 December 2020, accessed on 30 June 2023, https://www.who.int/news-room/fact-sheets/detail/the-top-10-causes-of-death

36 Centers for Disease Control and Prevention, 'Coronary Artery Disease', 19 July 2021, accessed on 24 May 2023, https://www.cdc.gov/heartdisease/coronary_ad.htm

The US National Stroke Association (disbanded in 2019) refers to several factors that may cause strokes:

- Medical risk factors like diabetes, high blood pressure, atrial fibrillation, high cholesterol, circulation problems
- Lifestyle risk factors like eating habits, physical activity, smoking and drinking
- Uncontrollable risk factors like ageing, gender and ethnicity

Death by stroke is the fifth highest cause of deaths in the US. Every four minutes, one person dies of stroke. The amazing fact is that that *80 per cent strokes are preventable*.[37]

The Cleveland Clinic clearly states that although risk factors for diabetes like family history cannot be changed, there are other factors that one can control. Implementing some of the lifestyle habits, like being healthy, staying physically active, avoiding smoking and drinking, reducing stress and getting proper sleep, can greatly help decrease the chances of getting type 2 diabetes. They go on to say that the chances of suffering from type 2 diabetes are greatly enhanced when one is overweight.

Did you find the culprit?

[37] WHO, 'Cardiovascular Diseases: Avoiding Heart Attacks and Strokes', 13 September 2015, accessed on 30 June 2023, https://www.who.int/news-room/questions-and-answers/item/cardiovascular-diseases-avoiding-heart-attacks-and-strokes

The answer is simple and so obvious but seemingly invisible. Simple because it is easy to understand and seemingly invisible because we have moved so far away from what should have been obvious to us. If you think diabetes is nothing too bad and not to be taken too seriously you must read the fact file given below:

During the Iraq and Afghanistan wars around 1,500 American soldiers lost a limb in combat.[38] During that same period, approximately 1.5 million Americans lost a limb due to amputation required as a consequence of type 2 diabetes.[39]

'Progress is impossible without change; and those who cannot change their minds cannot change anything.'—George Bernard Shaw

---

[38] Gary A. Cameron, 'Wounded War Veterans Find Brotherhood in Softball', Recovering As A Team, Reuters, Sports News, 28 May 2012, accessed on 30 June 2023, https://www.reuters.com/article/us-usa-veterans-amputees-idUSBRE84R02320120528

[39] Magdalena Walicka, Marta Raczyńska, Karolina Marcinkowska, Iga Lisicka, Arthur Czaicki, Waldemar Wierzba and Edward Franek, 'Amputations of Lower Limb in Subjects with Diabetes Mellitus: Reasons and 30-Day Mortality', National Library of Medicine, PubMed, 24 July 2021 accessed on 30 June 2023, https://pubmed.ncbi.nlm.nih.gov/34350296/#:~:text=Amputations%20in%20patients%20with%20diabetes%20accounted%20for%20a%20majority%20of,p%20for%20trend%20%3C%200.0000001.

How to Get on the Expressway of Good Health

3

Humans begin as a single cell which replicates itself into a trillion cells. But cells end up different due to their environments.[40] They are then wired differently so they can perform their varied functions. Thus, it is important to keep these cells healthy.

Micronutrients And Their Uses

Your expressway to good cell health is laden with sufficient

[40] Shyamala Iyer, 'Cell Division', Arizona State University School of Life Sciences, Ask A Biologist, 3 February 2014, accessed on 30 June 2023, https://askabiologist.asu.edu/cell-division

doses of vitamins and minerals. These play an important role in enhancing the quality and longevity of life.

Healthy ageing can be extended by ingesting optimal levels of thirty known micronutrients.This is because vitamins and minerals form key components of a vast number of different enzymes that are required by our cells to maintain the metabolic health of our body. Since we do not die an instant death due to a vitamin or mineral deficiency, we do not take them seriously.[41]

It should be no surprise that the same nutrients that keep us energized and happy on a daily basis, like vitamin D, omega-3 fatty acids and magnesium, are also critical components of enzymes required for our body's long-term maintenance. These nutrients are critical for DNA repair, cardiovascular health and prevention of oxidative damage. If we provide our cells with sufficient nutrients to take care of their immediate survival requirements as well as long-term needs (DNA repairs), they will be robust and strong enough to stave off diseases.

Why Is Supplementation Important?

Nutrients can be ingested as part of our diet. The natural ones we ingest with our food are the best. It is important to eat nutrient-rich food wherever and

---

[41] Bruce N. Ames, 'Prolonging Healthy Ageing: Longevity Vitamins and Proteins', National Library of Medicine, PubMed Central, 15 October 2018, accessed on 30 June 2023, https://www.ncbi.nlm.nih.gov/pmc/articles/PMC6205492

whenever possible. Unfortunately, supplementation has now become a necessity and is no longer a choice since the soil especially in India[42] is depleted of nutrients.

> ***'Unfortunately, supplementation has now become a necessity and is no longer a choice since the soil especially in India is depleted of nutrients.'***

Way back in 1998, the US National Academy of Sciences issued a report clarifying that even if one ate a good and healthy diet it would no longer provide our bodies with all its required nutrients.[43]

Today, the situation is far worse. The human genome has hardly changed from prehistoric times but our diets have been radically transformed. This in good measure is because our soil has got depleted of nutrients. To add to that, many nutrient-laden fruits and vegetables like the ansault pear, silphium have gone extinct.

Do we get adequate nutrients from the vegetables and meat we eat? The answer is NO. Our farm animals are just as sick and nutrient deficient as the rest of the food chain.

---

42 Anand P. Gupta, 'Micronutrient Status and Fertilizer Use Scenario in India', Science Direct, Journal of Trace Elements in Medicine and Biology, Volume 18, Issue 4, 27 June 2005, pp. 325-331, accessed on 30 June 2023, https://www.sciencedirect.com/science/article/abs/pii/S0946672X05000404

43 Dariush Mozaffarian, Irwin Rosenberg, Ricardo Uauy, 'History of Modern Nutrition Science—Implications for Current Research, Dietary Guidelines, and Food Policy', the bmj, Analysis, Science and Politics of Nutrition, 13 June 2018, accessed on 23 July 2023, https://www.bmj.com/content/361/bmj.k2392

This precarious situation is further acerbated since the food supply chain has become totally driven by economics. The combination of modern-day farming, harvesting (even before ripening), irradiating, refrigerating (sometimes for months/years) and shipping have greatly reduced the nutritional quality of the food we eat.

The situation in India is very similar to that around the West. Our soil is depleted of nutrients and it is just not good enough to keep us well and healthy.[44]

The ill effects of harvesting fruits and vegetables before they ripen are far worse than imaginable. Harvesting early increases the farmers' profits since it saves them losses caused by overripening of the produce. It also helps them get their produce to market for storage before rotting. What is overlooked though is that most fruits and vegetables develop a major part of their nutrients only one or two days prior to ripening. By harvesting ahead of time, we lose out on this critical phase which in some cases results in a loss of almost 80 per cent of nutrients that would have normally been added to the food chain.[45]

---

[44] Ishteyaque Ahmad, The Nutritional Imbalances in the Soil Are Causing Nutritional Depletion in Our Food, Greenpeace, 5 December 2021, accessed on 30 June 2023, https://www.greenpeace.org/india/en/story/12577/healthy-soil-for-healthy-us

[45] Sadat Kamal Amit, Md. Mezbah Uddin, Rizwanur Rahman, S. M. Rezwanul Islam and Mohidus Samad Khan, 'A Review on Mechanisms and Commercial Aspects of Food Preservation and Processing', BMC, Part of Springer Nature, Agriculture & Food Security, 21 November 2017, accessed on 30 June 2023, https://agricultureandfoodsecurity.biomedcentral.com/articles/10.1186/s40066-017-0130-8

I have not yet mentioned a word about the pesticides and herbicides that not only adversely affect the plants they are sprayed on, but also destroy the habitat of good bacteria, earthworms and snails that churn the earth and convert inorganic minerals in the soil into organically absorbable nutrients for plants. If the minerals are not in the soil, they cannot get into the plants and through them to us.

Spinach loses more than 50 per cent of its folic acid within three days of storage and broccoli loses more than 40 per cent of its vitamin C within a few days. These are just two examples. Imagine how much more is lost in cooking. [46]

Important Nutrients to Take

Doctors and health experts have time and again emphasized the importance of various minerals and vitamins for our health. A few are listed below:

Omega-3

Omega-3 is a fatty acid which the human body cannot produce,[47] so we must pick it up either from our food or

---

[46] 'Storage Time And Temperature Effects Nutrients In Spinach' Pennsylvania State University, Research 18 March 2005, accessed on 30 June 2023, https://www.psu.edu/news/research/story/storage-time-and-temperature-effects-nutrients-spinach

[47] Amber Charles Alexis, Fact Checked by Hilary Guite 'Omega-3: What It Can and Can't Do for Health', MedicalNewsToday, 10 December 2021, accessed on 23 July 2023, https://www.medicalnewstoday.com/articles/omega-3-what-it-can-and-cant-do-for-health

supplements. Omega-3 is commonly found in fatty fish like mackerels and salmon. It is also found in flax seeds, chia seeds, walnuts and almonds. Omega-3 promotes heart health by providing our body with good cholesterol, among other benefits.

Probiotics

Probiotics are live bacteria that may be consumed as supplements or as part of fermented foods like yogurt because they promote better digestion, weight loss, a tougher immune system and a stronger heart.

Vitamin D

Pain in the bones and muscle weakness indicate low vitamin D. A vitamin D deficiency can result in osteoporosis, bone fractures, bone pain and reduced stamina. Good exposure to sun can provide sufficient vitamin D but too much exposure can cause cancer. As with everything, you need to find a middle of the road approach. Like iron, calcium is also good for bone health, and dairy products are a rich source of this mineral.

Vitamin B12

Vitamin B12 plays a crucial role in DNA replication as well as in nerve cell regulation.[48]There is not much B12

[48] Alok, 'Vitamins & Supplements for Weight Loss: B12, Omega 3 & Magnesium', SK:N, 29 October 2021, accessed on 23 July 2023, https://www.sknclinics.co.uk/blog/vitamins-supplements-for-weight-loss-b12-omega-3-magnesium

in plant foods but it can be found in meats, eggs, poultry and shellfish. It is because of this, vegetarians and vegans must not miss out on B12 supplements.

Iron

Iron deficiency can make you feel tired, lethargic and weak. Many studies have proven that vitamin C helps in the absorption of iron.[49] Thus, eating foods that contain both vitamin C and iron works best. Like iron, calcium are also good for bone health, and dairy products are a rich source of this mineral.

Zinc

Zinc has a reputation of being a potent cold and flu virus antidote. Besides boosting immunity, zinc is essential for maintaining numerous physiological functions, including cellular growth, gut health and inflammation suppression.

Magnesium

Magnesium is critical for bone health and energy. Like iron, a deficiency in this mineral leads to a feeling of

---

[49] Restu Krisnanda, 'Vitamin C Helps in the Absorption of Iron in Iron Deficiency Anemia', Global Health Science Group, Archives, accessed on 26 May 2023, https://jurnal.globalhealthsciencegroup.com/index.php/JPPP/article/view/137

lethargy and fatigue. It also works as an electrolyte and its absence can cause severe cramps. Magnesium is also known to help one get sound sleep. It is found in pumpkin seeds where you could collect some zinc too.

Vitamin C

Vitamin C is essential for the growth and repair of tissues in our body. It helps with the formation of the important protein collagen, which is a critical component in our skin, cartilages, tendons, ligaments and even blood vessels. It is also important for healthy bones and teeth. Vitamin C may just be the wonder supplement. Papaya, kiwi, lemon and red pepper are all high in vitamin C.

What else may seem insignificant but can make a big difference to your life?

Important Lifestyle Habits That Improve Longevity

Four factors go a long way in improving your health and hence longevity.

Oral Hygiene

Latest research points to the possibility of gum disease bacteria causing Alzheimer's.[50]

---

[50] Jocelyn Kaiser, 'Gum Disease–Causing Bacteria Could Spur Alzheimer's', Science, 23 January 2019, accessed on 30 June 2023, https://www.science.org/content/article/gum-disease-

Physical Activity

Making the heart work harder through moderate to high intensity physical activity on a consistent basis helps lower blood pressure and improves heart health.

A Simple Stand

Sitting for an extended time has a negative impact on your heart, so it is important to take breaks by either walking for a minute or just standing to get the blood circulation going. You must stand up at least once in an hour.

Power Nap

Apart from a good night's sleep, a power nap of about twenty minutes is not only restorative to the body, but also results in better memory.

---

causing-bacteria-could-spur-alzheimers

The Retirement Myth Busted

4

We grow up, work hard and have a family. Then we work even harder to take care of our family until we turn sixty-five, retire and die. We do it because our parents did it. Our parents did it because their parents did it. Could it be that we have been programmed to function this way?

What is it that we all want? All over the world, we want the same things:

- A lot of money
- A long life and
- To be healthy forever

We are about eight billion unique individuals and yet most of us desire the same things. Can you see a pattern here? Could it be that we are programmed to think in a particular way?[51]

I have read extensively and researched for more than a couple of decades and I am of the considered opinion that we are all totally responsible for all that happens in our lives. We create all of our experiences based on how we think and feel. Our thoughts and words are enormously powerful.

What we think and speak find a way to the universe and come back to us as experience.

We Are All Victims of Victims

We all come into the world beautiful and innocent. Our software to interpret everything this world offers is downloaded into our minds by our parents, grandparents, caretakers, teachers, when we are very young. This is when we learn how we feel about ourselves and how to view life. Early childhood experiences from birth to the age eight affect the development of the brain's architecture, which provides the foundation for all future learning, behaviour and health. A strong foundation helps children develop the skills they need to become well-functioning adults.[52]

---

[51] Earl Nightingale, *The Strangest Secret*, Kindle edition, Larenzana Press, 2011.

[52] Centers for Disease Control and Prevention, 'Important Milestones: Your Child By Five Years', CDC, 6 December 2022, accessed on 25 May, https://www.cdc.gov/ncbddd/actearly/milestones/milestones-5yr.html

Very often, the thoughts we had and the decisions we took at that age were good for their times. They probably even helped us survive through childhood, but they were only good for that age and are unlikely to be effective in adult life. For example, I was warned not to whistle when walking home in the dark as it would attract evil ghosts. Now this made sense when I was young as it was not safe to attract attention to my 'small self' when walking down a lonely street in the dark, but to this day I think twice before whistling at night.

Very often, we learn these things when very young and unconsciously go on reinforcing them till we die. I believe that we are all victims of victims, so we should not blame our parents or mentors because they too were victims of victims and it was not possible for them to teach us something they did not know.

If your parents did not know how to love themselves, there was no way that they could teach you how to love yourself. If you grew up in a family that was very angry or frightened, it is likely that you maybe an angry and frightened person because that is what you learnt as a child. Now I am not sitting in judgement here but I am bringing to your attention certain facts.[53] Half the battle will be won once you develop an awareness of your situation.

The good news is that you can change it all. You have to learn to love yourself because it is only when we

---

[53] Louise Hay, 'How-To-Love-Yourself', accessed on 30 June 2023, https://www.louisehay.com/start-morning-routine-love

learn to love ourselves and acknowledge who we are in this time and space that little miracles begin to happen everywhere.[54] I am not talking about vanity. I am not encouraging you to be self-centred or selfish. I am just talking about appreciating the being that you are. You might want to do a lot of mirror work which I do with many of the people I mentor. I advise you do positive affirmations in front of a mirror in the morning. Stand in front of the mirror first thing in the morning and look yourself in the eye and lovingly tell yourself, 'I love you'. Then ask yourself in the mirror, 'What can I do today to make you happy?'

You may not get an answer for a while but if you do it consistently, you are likely to find a connection. This is a very healing thing to do. If nothing else just look into the mirror and say to yourself, 'I love you. I truly truly love you'. Because 'If you don't love yourself, nobody will. Not only that, you won't be good at loving anyone else. Loving starts with the self.' Bestselling author Dr Wayne Dyer could not have been more right.[55]

'Observe how babies are full of love and express themselves freely. They love their bodies from the top of their head to the tip of their toes including every point in between. They even love their own urine which they gladly play with and smear all over their bodies because nobody has taught them guilt and shame.

---

54 Osho, *The Dhammapada The Way of the Buddha*, Divyansh Publications, 1 January 2014.

55 Wayne W. Dyer, *Wishes Fulfilled*, Hay House Inc., 2013.

Then somewhere along the way you are sold this idea that you are not good enough and you start putting tape measures around your waistlines to see for yourself if you are acceptable and right for the world. As if that was not enough, the media dictates to you, how you are supposed to be of a certain weight or height before you become acceptable to your peers and others. Then the advertising industry tells you that you have to use a certain deodorant/perfume/toothpaste before you can be acceptable and loved. This just does not make sense especially since you are a wonderful and unique expression of God and magnificent divine expression of life itself. If you do not accept yourself the way you are, you are constantly trying to be like someone else all the while hoping that by doing that you will be more acceptable to others. In a nutshell, you are an innocent victim of well-meaning victims.

Many of your life's problems stem from the fact that 95 per cent of your life is lived based on the programs downloaded when you were less than five years old. It is only when you take control and shed your baggage that you will be able to move beyond your limitations.

Look at so many men and women who before retiring from a job look all energetic and happy but a few years into retirement look tired, lost, haggard and old. This is primarily because we have been programmed to think that retirement is the beginning of the end of our lives.

When, Where And How Did Retirement Start?

In earlier times, retirement was unheard of. Respect for the aged remained high and regardless of age, it was customary for them to carry on until they died. When a patriarch or matriarch could no longer farm, herd cattle or pitch a tent, they would opt for less labour-intensive work and move in with their children but retirement was unheard of.

As time passed and the longevity of life increased, the elderly population grew and by the early medieval period, their numbers became quite sizeable. After the Industrial Revolution, a bulk of jobs moved from farmlands to factories. The high speed of the industrial factories became difficult for the older workers to cope with resulting in a drop in overall efficiency, which put a strain on the economies of scale. Suddenly, the revered elderly became a burden to their loved ones.

All this remained quite unchanged until in 1883 when the Chancellor Otto von Bismarck was once again fighting to win the German national elections, but this time had his back pinned to a wall.[56] The only way he could win was if he could get the Marxists to back him. The Marxists agreed to support him on the condition that he would pay a monthly stipend to every unemployed German above the age of sixty-five. This is how the concept of retirement and the pension system was born. The age of sixty-five was quite random, political and hardly scientific. Whatever be the case it was fixed in the year 1883, but to this day continues to be more or less the same. In some places like India, it could even be as low as fifty-eight.

---

[56] Peter Feuerherd, 'Why Retirement Age Is 65 (And Why It's Getting Higher)', JSTOR Daily, 8 May 2017, accessed on 27 May 2023.

The retirement rules laid out by Chancellor Bismarck came in handy for the Americans. The second phase of the Industrial Revolution in the early 1900s left a large number of ageing unskilled factory workers unfit to work in factories since machinery speeds had increased drastically and accidents were becoming the norm. The elderly workmen simply could not keep pace with the high-speed machines and had become unacceptable liabilities on the salary bill. Pertinently they also blocked out younger, sturdy hands from being employed. The Great Depression made things even worse since costs had to be cut and efficiencies improved. Suddenly, retirement became a brilliant solution and a necessity. It became clear that the only way to get the inefficient and aged factory staff out of the way was to pay them a pension that would assure them of their upkeep and also encourage them to spend the rest of their days away from factories. It was in this context that President Franklin D. Roosevelt proposed the Social Security Act of 1935 and thus was born the concept of social security and retirement in the US.

Thus, the retirement age was fixed because the elderly were skilled differently. If we look ahead to the impending artificial intelligence revolution much the same thing is likely to happen. Many people will be forced to reskill or prematurely retire. This too will have nothing to do with age or health.

Isn't it shocking that the retirement age of around sixty-five years has been the same for more than a century despite the average life expectancy in countries like the UK and the US having more than doubled? In some cases, it has even dropped even though life expectancy has shot up! In India, the average life expectancy was a mere twenty-three a hundred years ago and has since more than tripled. So, the retirement age should have been raised by quite a few years.[57] If it was sixty-five in 1883, it should be at least eighty-five now.

I have no objection to those fifty-eight and above getting all the retirement benefits that they do. It is good for them. I feel happy that they get rewarded for giving many years of their lives in the service of humanity. However, I do have a problem when they retire and leave with the impression (which is ingrained into them from a very young age) that they are being laid off to pasture and die. It is strongly imprinted in their minds that they are too old to take on any serious responsibility or challenge. It leaves them with no reason to enjoy life.

This retirement myth is a major impediment in our quest for a long, healthy and happy life. It is a program that we need to wipe out of our brains as soon as possible. This program needs to be superimposed with a program of life.

It is because we imagine that we have been let out to pasture, that we bid our time to move on to the next world and our very thinking changes and we lose our sense of direction and belonging.

---

[57] Dhaval Dave, Inas Rashad and Jasmina Spasojevic, 'The Effects of Retirement on Physical and Mental Health Outcomes', National Bureau of Economic Research, NBER Working Paper Series, March 2006, accessed on 23 July 2023, https://www.nber.org/system/files/working_papers/w12123/w12123.pdf

- This thing called retirement steals our sense of purpose;
- It steals our reason to wake up in the morning;
- It knocks out all structures we had in our life;
- Retirement brings with it despair

How can we take control of our own lives and stave away the ill effects of retirement?

To Retire Is *Not* to Withdraw from Life

'Retire from work, but not from life.' M.K. Soni.

Retirement should not mean the end of the world. It is only the beginning of a different phase of our lives. It is only when we believe that we are not being let out to graze we will take up challenges that will keep us purposefully engaged. It is important to have a sense of purpose in life. It will give one a reason to wake up in the morning and put structure back in one's life. It is important to engage with society rather than withdraw into oblivion. Retirement is *not* a punishment. Someone had once said, 'Retirement is when you stop living at work and begin working at living.'

Studies now project humans can live for more than 125 years. They have even suggested that there is no fixed limit to human longevity. This is quite contrary to what demographers and biologists of old swore by.

According to the study of the extremely old Italians led by the University of California, Berkeley, and Sapienza University of Rome chances of reaching the ripe old age of 110 are within reach—if you survive the perilous 90s and make it to 105 when death rates level out.[58]

In a different study Elisabetta Barbi of Sapienza University and statistician Francesco Lagona of University of Roma found out in their research that the risk of death plateaued after the age of 105 creating a mortality plateau.[59] At that point, the odds of living beyond the next birthday were actually 50:50 making the possibility of unlimited longevity quite real. If there is a mortality plateau, there is a great possibility that there could actually be no limit to human longevity. Hypothetically, that would imply that someone who is 115 today could live for a few years to come or even forever.

The world houses in excess of five hundred thousand people who are aged more than 100.[60] The global number of centenarians should strongly increase during the twenty-first century. According to the Population

58 Yasmin Anwar, 'Odds of Living to 110-plus Level Out—Once You Hit 105', UC Berkley, 28 June 2018, accessed on 26 May 2023, https://news.berkeley.edu/2018/06/28/supercentenarians

59 Elisabetta Barbi, Francesco Lagona, Marco Marsili, James W. Vaupel, Kenneth W. Wachter,'The Plateau of Human Mortality—Demography of Longevity Pioneers', National Library of Medicine, PubMed Central, accessed on 18 June 2023, https://www.ncbi.nlm.nih.gov/pmc/articles/PMC6457902/,

60 Katharina Buchholz, 'There Are Now More Than Half a Million People Aged 100 or Older around the World', World Economic Forum, 17 February 2021, accessed on 27 May 2023, How Many Centenarians Are There Around the world? World Economic Forum (weforum.org)

Division of the United Nations, it should reach more than twenty-five million people in 2100.[61]

For James Kirkland, a geriatrician at the Mayo Clinic in Rochester, Minnesota, the strong evidence for a mortality plateau points to the possibility of forestalling death at any age. Some experts think that the very frail are beyond repair. But if the odds of dying do not increase over time, he says, interventions that slow ageing are likely to make a difference, even in the extremely old.[62]

Since longevity of the human life is on the increase, many scientists believe that living for more than 125 years is a serious possibility.[63] Keeping the above in mind, you must move forward with an open mind understanding very clearly that sixty-five is not by any means an age that should scare you or make you feel old or tired. Ageing can be controlled if we learn its dynamics. Old age need

---

[61] Jean-Marie Robine and Sarah Cubaynes, 'Worldwide Demography of Centenarians', Mechanisms of Ageing and Development, 165 (Part B), abstract, July 2017, accessed on 27 May 2023, Worldwide demography of centenarians—ScienceDirect

[62] Elie Dolgin, 'There's No Limit to Longevity, Says Study Reviving Human Life Span Debate', Scientific American, 1 July 2018, accessed on 27 May 2023, There's No Limit to Longevity, Says Study Reviving Human Life Span Debate - Scientific American

[63] Kim Eckart; 'How Long Can a Person Live? The 21st Century May See a Record-breaker', University of Washington, UW NEWS, 1 July 2021, accessed on 23 July 2023, https://www.washington.edu/news/2021/07/01/how-long-can-a-person-live-the-21st-century-may-see-a-record-breaker

not be the way most of us see it today.[64] It can be quite a happy and exciting part of our life if we take the trouble to look forward to it.

> ***'Since longevity of the human life is on the increase, many scientists believe that living for more than 125 years is a serious possibility.'***

This book seeks to build within you an awareness of the possibilities of life and how you should strive to live a long and happy life rather than spending almost all your savings on medical bills. A healthy, happy and long life is possible only if you start laying the foundations of your health beginning today because Rome was not built in a day. It will take persistence, determination, perseverance and focus to set right, firstly what you have been doing wrong for so many years and then to strengthen yourself for the long haul. Do not forget to plan for your very, very long journey. The thoughts you think and the words you speak are enormously powerful. Start thinking about how mental conditioning has been adversely affecting and limiting your life. And fix it.

Now that we know that we are victims of victims what do we do? You stop playing a victim.There is no limit to longevity. You can target to live 140 years.

[64] Emily Willingham, 'Humans Could Live up to 150 Years, New Research Suggests', Scientific American, 25 May 2021, accessed on 23 July 2023, https://www.scientificamerican.com/article/humans-could-live-up-to-150-years-new-research-suggests

Know the Chief Alchemist: Your Mind

5

Simply put, epigenetics is the study of how your behaviours and environment can cause changes that affect the way your genes work:

- The entire software on which our body runs is encapsulated in our DNA.[65] The human genome consists of approximately three billion nucleotides. The sequence of the base nucleotides could

[65] 'Deoxyribonucleic Acid (DNA) Fact Sheet', National Human Genome Research Institute, last updated: 24 August 2020, accessed on 23 July 2023, https://www.genome.gov/about-genomics/fact-sheets/Deoxyribonucleic-Acid-Fact-Sheet

determine your life's story.

- The human body is known to have around 19,000–20,000 genes, which carry within them instructions on how the body should create important proteins needed for our bodily functions. You will be awed when you understand how genes go about their work and also how the instructions they carry are influenced by their environment.

Our Lives Are Not Predetermined by Our Genes

In an experiment commonly conducted by scientists studying epigenetics, a single stem cell was taken from the human body and placed on a petri dish.[66] The required nutrients were provided. This single cell by the second day divided into two which went on to become four by the third day and so on till there were around 30,000 cells. All were from the same original one. These identical cells were then divided into three petri dishes. The only thing done was that the fluid into which the stem cells were placed (the environment) was different for each dish. The result was that the stem cells developed differently in the three petri dishes. One developed into skin cells and another into bone and so on.

---

[66] Craig Gustafson, Bruce Lipton, PhD, 'The Jump From Cell Culture to Consciousness', National Library of Medicine, PubMed Central, December 2017, accessed on 23 July 2023, https://www.ncbi.nlm.nih.gov/pmc/articles/PMC6438088

In our body, their environment is regularly changed by our mind. The brain sends different signals to the cells letting them know our body's needs based on what it perceives as required. Epigenetics determines what a cell will specialize in (for example, skin cells, blood cells, hair cells, liver cells, etc.). In a similar manner, epigenetics can also control how 'good' or 'bad' genes function. Epigenetics confirms our lives are not predetermined by our genes but by our mental make-up. Our mind is the chief alchemist.

Thus, your environment affects you and your health. What you eat and when you eat, where you live and how you live not only contribute to how long you live, but also how healthy and happy you will be. Could it be that if you take care of your immediate environment, you could turn off the genes that cause various sicknesses[67] like Alzheimer's, arthritis or Parkinson's? I believe you can even keep ageing at bay. Isn't it getting super mesmeric?

If there were a code to the longevity lock, this could be one of the combination numbers. Only till recently it was believed that we were destined to suffer from a particular disease if it was in our genes. We were sure nothing could be done if we inherited bad genes. We were victims of our destiny. Thanks to many studies we now know that the

---

67 Kenneth Olden, Nicholas Freudenberg, Jennifer Beam Dowd and Alexandra E. Shields, 'Discovering How Environmental Exposures Alter Genes and Could Lead to New Treatments for Chronic Illnesses', National Library of Medicine, PubMed Central, 1 January 2014, accessed on 23 July 2023, https://www.ncbi.nlm.nih.gov/pmc/articles/PMC3877678

genes that have the potential to cause havoc inside us can be turned off and those that can do us well can be turned on. Today we know that hibernating within our body are numerous monstrous genes but none of them are actively plotting against us until unknowingly we nudge them to life.

Another very simplistic way of looking at how epigenetics works is to think of the construction of the following simple sentence:

An English professor wrote the words: 'A woman without her man is nothing' on the chalkboard and asked her students to punctuate it correctly. All of the males in the class wrote: 'A woman, without her man, is nothing.'

All the ladies in the class wrote: 'A woman: without her, man is nothing.'

The same holds true for our genome. All cells in our body have the same DNA sequence. The differences in the 'punctuation' of the genes are what determine when they are turned on. This results in cells differentiating themselves into a broad array performing different functions. It is this that not only develops cells that turn into muscles, skin, nerves and bones but also form rogue cells that develop into cancer.

Can you imagine the enormity of this discovery and its impact on the healthy life span of the human race? To understand epigenetics from a different angle think of the difference in a cocktail that you would get if it were made by a professional mixologist and an inexperienced bartender using the same ingredients? Using the same ingredients and process the seasoned mixologist would make a cocktail to die for while the other one would be comparatively dull and insipid. This is one of the biggest secrets of life. In this context, the master chef is our mind and the environment is all about how our mind perceives our situation in this world at any given moment in time. If it continuously perceives us to be under threat it will respond by releasing the stress hormone cortisol[68] and if it perceives us to be at peace with the world it will release happy hormones like serotonin. Our body can handle stress hormones but if they are released over long periods of time they have the effect of turning on some rogue genes. Likewise, if happy hormones are secreted over a long period of time they are known to keep rogue genes turned off.[69]

Our Second Brain: The Gut

It is probably with good reason that our gut [70]is called our

---

[68] Mayo Clinic Staff, 'Chronic Stress Puts Your Health at Risk', Mayo Clinic Health Lifestyle, Stress Management, accessed on 2 July 2023, https://www.mayoclinic.org/healthy-lifestyle/stress-management/in-depth/stress/art-20046037

[69] Dariush Dfarhud, Maryam Malmir and Mohammad Khanahmadi, 'Happiness & Health: The Biological Factors—Systematic Review Article', National Library of Medicine, PubMed Central, November 2014, accessed on 2 July 2023, https://www.ncbi.nlm.nih.gov/pmc/articles/PMC4449495/#:~:text=Serotonin%20is%20a%20neurotransmitter%20that,serotonin%20available%20to%20brain%20cells

[70] Siri Carpenter, 'That Gut Feeling', The American Psychological

second brain. Notice how it plays a major role in our lives and in keeping our cells healthy.

Have you heard of this absolutely fascinating story of the Queen Bee?[71]

Royal jelly is a protein-rich jelly-like substance secreted by the nurse bees. All bee larvae are fed this jelly for a few days after hatching but the larva destined to become the queen bee is fed only royal jelly for her entire life inside a special enclosure called the queens cup. [72]To start off, the larvae that turn into worker bees and the larva that becomes the queen are genetically identical. They end up different only because they eat different food! While the larvae meant to be worker bees feed off a buffet of foods, the larva being brought up to be the queen bee is fed only royal jelly and nothing else. Unlike the others, this single larva goes on to develop ovaries and a larger abdomen for laying eggs. On the other hand, the worker bees eating a variety of food become sterile. The queen bee not only goes on to behave like one, but also sets out to kill any potential rival. After many experiments and much research, scientists concluded that the royal

---

Association, September 2012, accessed on 2 July 2023, https://www.apa.org/monitor/2012/09/gut-feeling

71 John Timbs, *The Curiosities of Bees*, Read Books, 2018.

72 Gwen Pearson, 'Royal Jelly Isn't What Makes a Queen Bee a Queen Bee', 2 September 2015, Wired, https://www.Wired.Com/2015/09/Royal-Jelly-Isnt-Makes-Queen-Bee-Queen-BEE/#:~:TEXT=A%20DEVELOPING%20QUEEN%20BEE%20IS,PERHAPS%2C%20FOOD%2COF%20GENETIC%20MONARCHIES

jelly turned off a key gene (*Dnmt3*), which codes for an enzyme that silences a group of 'queen genes'. When the bees stop feasting on the royal jelly, *Dnmt3* is turned on and the queen genes are epigenetically silenced, by default turning the larvae into a worker. But when royal jelly keeps *Dnmt3* 'switched off', the queen genes remain active, turning single larva from the same family into a queen bee.

Healthcare System or Disease Management System?

Would it still be right to say that there are serious genetic diseases that cannot be avoided? Yes, but one would probably be referring to less than 5 per cent of all. However, we should accept responsibility for the 95 per cent. There is no compelling reason why people should suffer from so many of the commonly known chronic diseases.

Have you abdicated your duty towards yourself and handed over responsibility of your health to others?

If yes, you need to immediately reclaim responsibility for your health. There are many powerful corporations that would do anything to be in control of your health. Many not in a very altruistic way. They would like to make you feel slightly better only to enable you to live longer so as to increase your dependence on them.

Does our existing healthcare system really maintain our health? The answer to that question is a resounding NO. It waits for you to fall sick and then treat the symptoms. It is the symptoms that most of our doctors are trained to manage. If you suffer from high blood pressure, you are prescribed pills to lower it. If you suffer from high blood sugar, you are prescribed tablets to lower it. Patients are told to have these tablets continuously increasing the doses as they age. The health care system as we know it generally does not cure you of chronic disease. In many ways it keeps one alive but only to suffer later. The current health care system could better be called a disease management system.

'Health is your choice. It is your responsibility and not your doctors', parents' or children's.'

This is why I urge you to take personal responsibility for your health. Health is your choice. It is your responsibility and not your doctors', parents' or children's. Even though this is so important for us no school or college ever teaches us how to go about it. This should be the most important course in the school syllabus. But it isn't. Any guess why?

Understanding the Placebo Effect And the Nocebo Effect

This takes me to a true story of Elisha Perkins (16 January 1741–6 September 1799), a physician and well-known healer. A Connecticuter,[73] he practised

[73] William Snow Miller, 'Elisha Perkins and His Metallic Tractors', National Library of Medicine, PubMed Central, Yale Jr. Biol. Med., October 1935, accessed on 2 July 2023, https://www.ncbi.nlm.nih.gov/pmc/articles/PMC2601307/?page=1

medicine with great success. His practice was the envy of many, especially his peers. During the late eighteenth century, in keeping with the perceived advancements in medicine patients expected more effective therapies. Physicians were forced to hone their skills to meet these expectations. Around 1795, Perkins was awarded a fourteen-year patent for an invention he called Tractors. The tractors consisted of two three-inch metal rods with a pointed end. Despite being made of only steel and brass, Perkins pompously announced that they were made of very unusual metal alloys. He used these tractors to cure rheumatism, headaches, inflammation and even facial pains. Tractor points were applied on the patient's aching body part by passing the pointed edges over them for about twenty minutes. In Perkins words, the tractor rods would 'draw out noxious electrical fluid that was at the root of suffering'.

As is always the case with great success, Perkins was also followed by many sceptics. While critics derided the tractors as fake and a few called the inventor a quack the citizenry as a whole hero-worshipped him. Elisha Perkins countered his critics with charges of elitism and professional arrogance. He boasted of more than 5,000 cured cases. These cures were certified by professors, physicians and clergymen. Even George Washington bought a set of tractors. This gave Perkins the opportunity to proclaim, 'The President of America bought the tractors only because he was convinced of the efficacy of the treatment as it was successfully used to treat his own family.'

But another highly respected physician John Haygarth was convinced that Perkins was pulling a fast one and challenged the popular treatment.

While going about his investigation Dr Haygarth decided to prepare a pair of tractors resembling the original ones and decided to keep it a secret. He insisted that the effects of both the false tractors and the genuine ones should be reported and recorded in the words of the patients.

Armed with this plan Dr Haygarth and his friend Dr Falconner procured two wooden tractors of nearly identical shape as the original metallic ones and made them perfectly to resemble the originals. Five patients suffering from chronic rheumatism in the ankle, knee, wrist and hip were selected from the General Hospital. One of the patients also had gout pains. On 7 January 1799, the two medico-adventurists set off to prove a point to the world. When the shortlisted patients were exposed to the use of the wooden tractor, all but one profusely thanked the doctors for their pain was relieved. Lest you think the wooden tractors were pressed into the muscle of the convalescent so as to physically have a massage-like effect on the patient, they were not. The wooden tractors were drawn over the skin only so as to touch it in the slightest manner as would be done by Dr Perkins' tractors.

The next day, Perkins' metallic tractors were used and the results were very similar to the fake ones. Similar trials were also conducted by other doctors and recorded.

Dr Haygarth was delighted to announce his findings. He claimed, 'This method of discovering the truth distinctly proved to what a surprising degree mere fancy deceives the patient himself.'

This is how John Haygarth proved that our imagination was all-powerful. Such is the power of your mind. Such is the power of your thoughts.

From the eighteenth century, let us now fast forward to the twentieth.

This is a true story that actually happened to me somewhere in the year 1998 when I was highly overweight. I had become a prolific swimmer. I could swim for an hour at a stretch and I did this for quite a while. One day on a cold and dull morning when alone in the pool, I suddenly felt a strong pain in my chest, it felt as if God was calling. I panicked, developed cold sweats and rushed out. By the time I got out, I realized there were two roads ahead that could lead me to my destiny. One was an expressway to my maker while the other was a life filled with medicines, pokes and pricks and all that came with frequent visits to the doctor. I was young and simply was not ready to accept the possible change. Rather stupidly, I went to the changing room and did a few sit-ups. This I thought would speed up my meeting with my Creator! I did not want to live on earth with a body that was not functioning well. I was relieved that I did not collapse, so my body was not in that bad shape after all. A few days later when I was not feeling well, I went to my physician for a check-up and he recommended me for a stress test. The stress test was positive and I was advised to go for an angiogram. The few days between the episode in the swimming pool and the angiogram were like driving in the mountains with sharp bends at dusk on a rainy day.

I was the chemist at my family's distillery and whenever I left town for a few days it was my job to delegate the blending of various products to my assistant after I blended the secret portions and left the mixes with him. That way manufacturing in my absence would continue unhindered. To mix these secret portions, I would have to lift a couple of bottles which weighed one or two kilos each. For me this was a routine and I would do it without a thought; however, now that I had a 'heart condition' every time I lifted a bottle I would feel a dull ache in the left side of my chest. My hand would feel limp and it would be very difficult for me to even lift a bottle. Anyway, armed with a few prayers and feeling sorry for myself I finished off my job and grudgingly was ready to go for the angiogram to Bengaluru with the dreaded anticipation that this was just the beginning of years of struggle, trauma and adjustment. I wasn't really happy to be alive in this condition but felt I had a responsibility to hang on since I was needed by my dear wife, two sweet daughters and my ageing parents.

The angiogram was a wonderful anticlimax. It was the first time I had got into an operation theatre and having been given an injection was waiting to drift off to sleep when the doctor told me to expect a sudden hot flush through my body. Before I knew it, he had almost finished the procedure. I could not believe my ears when he pronounced that there was nothing wrong with me and I was as fit as a fiddle. Within minutes, I was feeling fine and energized. I was ready to party! Nothing had changed. The same sick me of a few minutes ago had miraculously become a strong and energized human being without any medication whatsoever!

Dr Haygarth was a man who understood the placebo effect well. That day at the swimming pool and the days that followed I was going through what is called the nocebo effect, which is the opposite of the placebo effect. The term nocebo comes from the Latin 'to harm'. Nocebo implies that patients are more likely to experience an adverse effect if they expect or are worried about the adverse effect. I imagined the worst was wrong with me and my body adjusted itself to feel that way. If I had not got the correct information by doing the angiogram, with time my body could have probably generated the blocks only to justify my thinking and meet my expectations. I will dwell on it in more detail.

A placebo is a medical treatment or procedure designed to deceive the participant of a clinical experiment or treatment. The medicine does not contain any active ingredients but often still produces a physical effect on the subject. It is because the mind can influence how medication can affect us that placebos are now being used on a routine basis to confirm the efficacy of drugs.

The placebo effect has been observed and measured in thousands of medical cases. Because of its proven benefits many doctors openly prescribe placebos.

Interestingly, placebo effects are seen to vary depending on numerous factors.[74] A distilled water injection results in a stronger placebo effect than a dummy tablet. Two dummy tablets are known to show better results than one and capsules are seen as more potent than tablets. Larger pills produce better results! Studies have even confirmed that even colours of pills make a difference to their effect. For example, red, orange and yellow are associated with a stimulating effect while blue and green colours have a soothing effect.

Why am I describing the placebo effect to you?

Well, it is an interesting phenomenon and more importantly in the present context it is paramount so that you understand and accept the importance of your mind and what it can do to you. A happy mind can catapult your body into a healthy state which in turn will keep illness at bay and similarly a sad, pessimistic and negative mind can do the reverse.

I call it the wheel of health. We fall sick so we go to the doctor who gives us a pill that puts us right but makes us toxic so we go back to be treated for the resultant side effects and the cycle is never ending. Allow me to demystify this very complex phenomenon we call health. Covid-19 is an exception, so I will not discuss it.

[74] Fabrizio Benedetti, Elisa Carlino and Antonella Pollo, 'How Placebos Change the Patient's Brain', Nature, Neuropsychopharmacology, 30 June 2023, accessed on 2 July 2023, https://www.nature.com/articles/npp201081

The WHO says there are more than 12,500 known diseases around the world. The very thought of having to manage these many sicknesses terrifies us into giving up. Let me simplify this for you.

Let us take the example of your mobile phone, which you need to charge daily. The same is true for our body which rejuvenates and repairs itself when we are asleep. In the morning, we wake up good as new. If you get biologically older at the same rate you get chronologically old, it is not good but you could at least consider it to be fair. Unfortunately, some people can get three or even ten days older overnight. At times, it is even more. That is neither fair nor normal and should not be taken lightly. It is common to see thirty-year-olds become fifty biologically. Ideally, we should be targeting to make fifty-year-olds biologically thirty. In a nutshell, we have it all mixed up.

The solution to this situation is obvious. You just need to accept the fact that your body is a self-repairing system.[75] Your only job is to keep it that way—self-repairing. You have to be the supplier of the repair material. These supplies are most important. When you get this balance right, you will remain biologically young,

---

[75] Kuei-Hui Chu, Heng-Hsin Tung, Daniel L. Clinciu, Hua-I Hsu, Yi-Chen Wu, Ching-I Hsu, Shu-Wei Lin and Shi-Jun Pan, 'A Preliminary Study on Self-Healing and Self-Health Management in Older Adults: Perspectives From Healthcare Professionals and Older Adults in Taiwan', National Library of Medicine, PubMed Central, 24 March 2023, accessed on 2 July 2023, https://www.ncbi.nlm.nih.gov/pmc/articles/PMC8958667

if you get it wrong you will get it all messed up.[76]

The person whose reflection you see in the mirror in front of you is not a single body but a collection of more than fifty trillion individual cells. Each of these cells is a microscopic unit of life. You started life as a single cell in your mother's womb and grew to be a community of cells collectively acting together for your survival and betterment. If all cells functioned perfectly, you would be in perfect health. It is only when some cells do not function well that you become unwell. Keeping this in mind it would not be wrong to say that disease is nothing but a manifestation of malfunctioning cells. The more cells malfunction the sicker we get. This brings us to the next logical questions: Why do cells malfunction?

And what can you do to correct this situation?

The answer is absolutely simple—all you need to do is to heal your malfunctioning cells and bring them back to normal. It is safe to say that more than 95 per cent of your cells would function normally if all their needs are met. It is your primary responsibility to supply your cells with what they require for maintenance and find a way to keep your body from adding toxins that will make the repairs difficult.

There are only two reasons for a cell to malfunction: Either it is deficient in something it needs to function optimally or there is a toxin which is obstructing its functioning. Making the following adjustments will help bring you back into the rejuvenate mode:

[76] Raymond Francis, *Never Be Sick Again: Health Is a Choice, Learn How to Choose*, Health Communications Inc., 2002.

1. Reduce your toxic load by reducing your intake of
    - sugar
    - wheat
    - processed oils
    - dairy products
    - pesticides
2. Mentally connect to the universe and keep your mind free from toxic thoughts. Just like what you eat and drink has an effect on your body, so also what you put into your mind affects your body. Good thoughts give you good results and bad thoughts give you bad results.
    - Do away with stress
    - Banish anger
    - Bury jealousy/envy
    - Start with meditation
3. Keep your body safe and exercise it well. It facilitates the delivery of nutrients and assists with the removal of toxins.
4. Take supplements. Keep the supplies to the cells at optimal levels. Remember, supplies are critical.
5. You are not a robot. You need to stop thinking of yourself as a robot whose parts can be changed. One often looks at it that way—if a leg goes bad substitute it with an artificial one; if a liver goes bad do a transplant. I would rather you look at yourself as an iPad—if you have a problem, connect to the web called the universe and download the proper software.
6. Genes are important and can be improved. The genetic activity varies constantly, and responds to

the input we give our body. The old thinking that we are governed by our genes and in that sense are helpless is absolutely wrong. Your thoughts control them.

7. Medicine has done a lot for disease control and the longevity of life; however, it needs to do a lot to fix the root of the problem. Be aware of this when you pop pills mindlessly.

You only have one body. You have NO *second chance.*

- When alive, we believe we do not have enough money to spend.
- When already in heaven, our money is still in the bank.
- Why are we so busy making so much money at the cost of not having time for ourselves?
- Are we slogging only to pay medical bills as we age?

God has given us one body and we just tend to take it all for granted. This argument holds true even if you do not believe in God. We are not discussing religion here, but the fact is that you have only one body for your entire lifetime. You may use it as you will. You could do a good job of it or you could abuse and destroy it.

I remember when I was a chain-smoker and people would warn me that I would get cancer or have a heart attack. I would contradict them with obscure facts and figures to justify my smoking. I would talk about all my non-smoking friends who had died of heart attacks and lung cancer. Even a teetotaller can suffer from liver cirrhosis. Regarding being overweight, I would always desire to lose weight, but I would always justify my eating and drinking as my way of life. I would refuse to change my lifestyle since I confused it with my personality. But then being true to oneself is also important. But what does 'lifestyle' really mean?

We may be able to justify to others our weakness for unhealthy food, drinks and even justify our inability to exercise, meditate or be healthy but *the least we must do is be truthful to ourselves*. For this, we need to reflect. We need to remind ourselves that we need to live in our bodies for a very very long time! It makes sense to keep it healthy. In the long run, no amount of wealth can make a sick man happy. While reflecting, depending on your age, decide how you would like to be when you are 40/ 50/ 60/70/80/90/100/110/120/130 and even 140. It does not happen by chance, we have to work towards it. You have the option of feeling like a forty-year-old when sixty, or you could be aching all over and feeling like a ninety-year-old when only sixty. While some of this is dependent upon the Creator quite a bit of it is in our hands. There are so many physically fit people who have suffered heart attacks and died but should we be talking of them or the happy, healthy living ones?

All through the time when I was gaining weight, I did not even notice it. This was probably because I was not looking into the mirror objectively. We have to make a conscious effort to look out for our flaws. To succeed, it is imperative to look at ourselves objectively. If you are looking to lose weight and do not want to sit with a pen and paper and audit what goes into your mouth, it is fine. I have lost more than 27 kg but have never been able to get myself to do a food audit. But most weight loss programmes recommend this as a first step. I was not prepared to let someone else take control of my life. I needed to do it my way. I had to find a way by which I would enjoy losing weight and laugh my way through weight loss. I needed to find a way by which I could continue to drink, eat and party as I was used to, only now I would do it fully conscious of what I was putting into my mouth. It would be about getting conscious by looking at the bigger picture of good health, longevity, happiness and bliss rather than doing a painstaking food audit which would have been aweful. Believe me, I was confident that I would party much harder than I had done in the recent past and enjoy much more than I had in the years gone by. After all, feeling younger is like living life all over again.

Rewire your mind. Follow my experience, it will smoothen the road for you. I consciously started looking into the mirror while all the time reminding myself to be objective. I had this (do you have it too?) subjective way of looking at myself and hoodwinking myself into believing that I was pretty handsome.

The best way to go about this fairly is to look into the mirror as if you were a stranger. Only then would you be able to look at yourself objectively. We always look at others the way they are, don't we? After this new way of objectively looking at myself there were times I would see in me a potential sumo wrestler! There was a hell of a lot of flab falling over from all directions. But here lay a catch. The sumo wrestlers were much tougher than me since they had super-strong muscles too. That was something I just did not have. All I had was a lot of flab. I realized that I needed to do something about my weight. I could not simply go about blowing up my life irresponsibly. I was not getting younger and this could be my last chance to shape up before I was forced to by the medical fraternity that in many cases could be ever so happy to have an additional patient to practise on.

God had blessed me with good health and I was not just about to blow it all up by putting more crap into my mouth. My skin was stretched to what now suddenly felt like its limit. I actually imagined that if a pin pricked my ballooned calf muscles they would burst open. The stretch marks were obvious and getting worse. I was sure that my output on the treadmill was also down. This was because I exercised a bit but went on eating and drinking much more than a normal average human being needed to.

As part of this 'awareness building' programme of mine, I began to notice that at times even my big car felt small. I became aware that it was I who was actually becoming bigger and not the car getting smaller. I received another nudge when I went to the US on a holiday with my family. We went out shopping but none of the clothes fited me. The number of obese persons in the States is quite high, so I was confident that finding a shirt of my size would not be too difficult. But my experience made me realize that I was entering a seriously dangerous territory. God sends messengers. You only have to look out for them. Mine were the people fatter than me. I saw in them a reflection of my future if I did not control and reverse my situation urgently. The more I saw such super-obese people the more I wanted to change.

Brainwash yourself by building an awareness of your reality as I did. It does not matter if your problem is obesity, a poor diet, addiction or anything else. It works wonders. It worked for me. It will work for you. Importantly, you will be able to do what you want to do, drink what you want to and when you want to, eat what you want to and when you want to and still be healthy along the way. Above all, build an awareness of your good friend Mr Sugar. He is an evil friend you need to put away.

'Whatever the mind can conceive and believe in, it can achieve.' Napoleon Hill

Best-selling author Napoleon Hill has guided more people to success than any other known person in the world. He is someone I have followed for many years and I am happy to share with you his words of wisdom as brought out in his popular book *Think and Grow Rich*.

Napoleon Hill was clear that desire was the stepping stone to success in whatever we set out to achieve. Be it weight loss, happiness, good health, riches or long life. You should not set off on a journey of more than a hundred years only with a wish to live a healthy happy life. Forget about more than a hundred years, you should not even set off on a weight loss programme with only a hope to lose weight. That would be wishful thinking. You will succeed only if you have a burning desire to achieve your goal.

Six Practical Steps to Achieve Longevity

The method by which a desire for a long life may be transmuted into reality consists of the following:

Fix the Exact Age You Wish to Live

It is not enough that you say that you wish to live a long life. You must be definite and clear in your mind as to how many years you wish to enjoy a healthy and happy life. That exact number is more important than just an abstract idea as it becomes a concrete thing and not just wishful thinking.

Determine Exactly What You Will Give Up For a Healthy Life

Nothing in this world comes free. You always have to pay a price for everything you desire. Determine exactly what you will give up for the healthy life. You could decide the amount of time per day you dedicate to health which could be in the form of joining a gym, cutting off sugars from your diet, reading a book to relax, etc. It will have to be multi-pronged else it will get boring and with time you will give up. Nothing comes free—*you must be ready to pay an equitable price.*

Fix Milestones

If you decide to lose weight, improve your diet, cut down on sugar, start meditation and then set out a timeline to follow. Set milestones to follow your progress. Where practicable, as in the case of weight loss, set goals based on a timeline. Be realistic about your goals to give yourself a fighting chance of success. If your goal is too easy, it will not be challenging and exciting and if it is too utopian, you will soon lose interest and give up. Keep your objectives realistic but challenging.

Create a Plan

Put together a plan. You could go and get yourself a gym membership or buy yourself a treadmill or a pair of walking shoes. You could even do something as simple and inexpensive as giving up all sugars for the next forty-five days starting immediately or you could join a yoga class. You could even start with supplements. Whatever you do, you *must make a plan and start immediately*.

Write Down a Concise Statement of Your Plan

For example, if weight loss is your immediate goal, write out a brief statement of how much weight you intend to lose and by when. Also, add precisely what you will give up. Describe clearly the plan which will help you achieve your goal. This looks simple but it is a very important step.

Read Aloud This Statement Several Times

Read aloud your statement at least twice daily. Once before retiring for the day, and again soon after waking up in the morning. As you read, feel and believe that you have already lost your desired weight, you will start feeling healthy and strong. See, feel and believe that you have already lost weight *but do not stop working at it.*

If you truly desire to lose weight and are obsessed with it, you should have no problem in convincing yourself that you will attain your weight loss goal.

Just in case you think this is hocus pocus and are not prepared to engage in these mind games, let me remind you that this theory is not mine and it is not even an untested one. It has been developed based on a theory regarding accumulation of great wealth laid out by one of the world's greatest business magnets Andrew Carnegie who shared it with his friend Napoleon Hill. This theory has been tested and found true for everything that a human being desires—even a long and healthy life. You might as well know that you will never ever be able to cross 100 unless you work on yourself to achieve lasting good health. The one quality that you will need to win is definiteness of purpose which will give you clarity regarding how far you wish to go and then combined with a burning desire to go for it.

I am reminded of Arnold Schwarzenegger, who was utterly broke when he was young. He was not-so-good-looking, weak-bodied man from war-torn Austria who had a burning desire to star in Hollywood movies. He moved to the US and spent many months working out in a gym for five hours a day. He was repeatedly dismissed by Hollywood as unemployable. To add to this, he was often ridiculed for his bad accent, but he persisted. Suddenly one day, most unexpectedly, he was given a role in *Hercules*, then came *The Terminator* and without anyone even knowing, a great star was born. The same man born with an awkward body, chipped at it until he became a superstar.

Schwarzenegger was successful only because he had a clear and definite goal, he had a burning desire to achieve it and he was ready to pay the price to achieve his goal. Before you go to the next chapter, go back to the six steps mentioned above, and work on them.

Write out a concise statement of what you will achieve in the coming five years. Set out a time-bound road map to follow. Add precisely what you will give up to achieve your goal.

Remember

- Every morning remind yourself that your mind is your chief alchemist. Be aware of the thoughts you think and the words you speak. They are enormously powerful.
- What you eat and when you eat, where you live and how you live determine how long you live and also how healthy and happy you will be.
- You have an almost perfect body that can even handle stress hormones but only if they are not released continuously over long periods of time. In stressful times, make it a point to take a break.
- Your gut is your second brain. It plays a major role in keeping your cells vibrant and healthy. Look after it.
- You have it within you to control more than 95 per cent of the disease that come your way. You must

first accept that you are the only one responsible for your own well-being. If you have abdicated this duty towards yourself and handed it over to your doctor, you need to immediately reclaim your responsibility. You have the option of feeling like a forty-year-old when sixty or you could be aching all over and feeling like a ninety-year-old when only sixty.

'Lovely days don't come to you. You should walk to them.'—Rumi

Know Your Second Brain: The Gut

6

Why We Eat When We Do?

What makes us feel hungry and why are we not most hungry when we wake up after probably the longest 'fast' between dinner and breakfast? It is a lot about Circadian rhythms.[77]

Circadian rhythms are twenty-four-hour cycles of changes in behaviour which are the result of hormonal and glandular activity. Most hormones secreted by our

[77] Courtney M. Vaughn and Bradley V. Vaughn, 'Encyclopedia of Sleep and Circadian Rhythms', ScienceDirect, 2023, accessed on 2 July 2023, https://www.sciencedirect.com/topics/neuroscience/hormonal-rhythms

body are secreted based on this cycle. The most obvious hormone to be released in circadian rhythm is the sleep hormone, melatonin. It is most active in the dark. Due to melatonin's sensitivity to light, you must lie in a dark room to get a good night's sleep. That is why you have a disturbed sleep if you do not switch off the lights before going to bed.

Important hormones like cortisol, growth hormone, the hunger hormone ghrelin are all secreted based on a circadian rhythm.[78] These patterns are seen in all animals including humans. They have evolved and they change in sync with the time of day and the seasons of the year. Going back 70,000 years, man was a hunter-gatherer. He would hunt only what he saw and that would be in the daylight since it was both difficult to catch prey in the dark as well as dangerous for him to be out hunting at night as he would not be able to defend himself against predators that would roam free and unnoticed. Nocturnal animals have their circadian rhythms tuned differently and therefore are awake at night. They are also more comfortable eating at night. These animals would happily eat up a human being as prey. As a result, humans would as a rule hunt by day and eat before sunset.

---

[78] Tae Won Kim, Jong-Hyun Jeong and Seung-Chul Hong, 'The Impact of Sleep and Circadian Disturbance on Hormones and Metabolism', National Library of Medicine, PubMed Central, 11 March 2015, accessed on 2 July 2023, https://www.ncbi.nlm.nih.gov/pmc/articles/PMC4377487

When Should You Have Your Biggest Meal?

Equipped with this information, I started scanning for studies that showed significant differences between people that followed their circadian rhythm and ate more in the daylight and very little at night and those who ate a heavy and late dinner. Among many research papers,[79] I found an interesting one that studied two groups. Both groups were given to eat 1,400 calories a day of the same food. The only difference was that one group had breakfast as its main meal while the other group's main meal was dinner. While the macronutrient content for both groups was identical, the timing of the largest meal differed. Since their daily calorie intake was restricted to only 1,400 calories, both groups lost weight but the one that ate a heavy breakfast and little at night lost much more than the one that ate a light breakfast and a heavy meal at night.

Why? On investigation it was found that the pancreas responded differently to the two groups. Insulin released after the big breakfast was much less than after the big dinner. The same number of calories from identical food resulted in two different responses from the pancreas only based on the timing of the feed. Research shows that insulin is a driver of weight gain and this explains why

---

[79] Daniela Jakubowicz, Maayan Barnea, Julio Wainstein and Oren Froy, 'High Caloric Intake at Breakfast vs Dinner Differentially Influences Weight Loss of Overweight and Obese Women', National Library of Medicine, PubMed Central, accessed on 2 July 2023, https://pubmed.ncbi.nlm.nih.gov/23512957

the group that ate a larger dinner lost less weight than the one that ate a larger breakfast. Unlike what we generally think, weight gain is not only the result of excess calories, but also affected by when we eat. It is not difficult to infer that we should eat lighter at night for better weight management. Incidentally, even though they did not have science to back them up many of our ancestors instructed us to eat early since from their experience one could sleep better on a light stomach. They were not wrong when they opined that an early dinner would help our food get digested before bed so it would not get accumulated in our gut as fat. While their science may not have been very accurate, we now know that due to our circadian rhythms it is healthy for us to dine early. Despite not eating for long hours after dinner, why is hunger the lowest in the morning? In line with our circadian rhythm, the ghrelin levels are at their lowest at 9 a.m.[80] Therefore, we are least hungry when we wake up and not really hungry at breakfast time. Most of us eat a hearty breakfast because we have been told that it is the most important meal of the day. However, I could not find any big study to justify it. If we go by the premise that our body knows its needs, we would not be wrong in inferring that since hunger is least in the morning our body clock is signalling us not to eat too much at breakfast time. Since insulin at night is

[80] Jason Fung, medically reviewed by Bret Scher, 'How to Not Get Hungry: Fasting and Ghrelin', Diet Doctor, 20 April 2017, accessed on 14 January 2024, https://www.dietdoctor.com/not-get-hungry-fasting-ghrelin

higher than during the day, it is obvious that we should not eat too much at night either. That leaves us with an afternoon window for our largest meal.

Incidentally, this is what the highly rated Mediterranean diet recommends. Italians, who are known to be healthier than most, often eat a large meal at lunch, follow it with a siesta and only a heavy snack for dinner. So the Mediterranean diet is healthy not only due to the foods, but also because of the timing of the heavy meal of the day.

For many, having a heavy lunch may not always be practical since evening often brings the family together for a family meal which tends to be heavy. It is also the time when most social gatherings take place. One would have to strike a balance knowing fully well the implications of one's decision.

So you now know that you do not have everything under your control and that the universe has even provided you with a hidden clock that you must learn to follow.

Our body shape is not only governed by what we eat, but also by the state of our gut.

Do you know that you are a holobiont?[81] Allow me to introduce you to your other side! This is not a joke. In terms of number of cells in your body, your cells are

---

[81] Brian Lovett, 'Does the Holobiont Add Crucial Context or Irrelevant Complexity?', American Society for Microbiology, 1 October 2021, accessed on 2 July 2023, https://asm.org/Articles/2021/October/Does-the-Holobiont-Add-Crucial-Context-or-Irreleva

outnumbered by the bacterial cells you carry by a factor of 1:10. Just to clarify, you carry ten times more microbe cells than your own.

The number of genes of microbes in your microbiome is more than 200 times your own gene pool.

You carry more than trillions of microbes in and on your person.[82] That is what makes you a Holobiont!

If you have understood the ramifications of the above, you are probably not only looking out for a good disinfectant to wash yourself with but also on the lookout for a good antibiotic to kill and flush out all microbes from your body. Do not be in a big hurry to do that. Even though we have always looked at bacteria and fungi as bad for health and tried our best to get 'rid of them', they are not all bad. Indeed, most of the microbes we carry are good.

Gut Bacteria: How It Can Make or Break You

All over our body, be it inside it or outside, we carry more than trillions of microbes including bacteria, archaea, fungi, viruses and microbes. Together, all these form our microbiota based on which is formed our microbiome which consists of the total gene pool in the microbiota.

---

[82] Elakshi Dekaboruah, Mangesh Vasant Suryavanshi, Dixita Chettri and Anil Kumar Verma, 'Human microbiome: an academic update on human body site specific surveillance and its possible role', Springer Link, 10 June 2020, accessed on 2 July 2023, https://link.springer.com/article/10.1007/s00203-020-01931-x

However, both terms are frequently used to mean the same thing. Whatever the name, please be warned that this thing called the microbiome can make or break you.

‘Even though we have always looked at bacteria and fungi as bad for health and tried our best to get “rid of them”, they are not all bad.’

Many researchers have even dubbed the microbiome a ‘forgotten organ’. While others have even called it the ‘second brain’. It could be the key link between our brain and the rest of cur body which controls obesity, cardiovascular disease, Alzheimer’s, diabetes and many other sicknesses.

The ecosystem in our microbiome is as diverse as the Amazon forests [83]with thousands of species all doing their ‘own thing’, but symbiotically and unknown to them they actually perform different functions for our body. The bacteria in our gut helps digest food, they produce vital vitamins like B12, riboflavin, thiamine and even vitamin K which are important and help with coagulation of blood. Did you know that almost 90 per cent of serotonin, our happy chemical, is produced in our gut? In babies, the microbiome even produces enzymes that help them

---

[83] Jose Pedro Fonseca, Luisa Hoffmann, Bianca Catarina Azeredo Cabral, Victor Hugo Giordano Dias, Marcio Rodrigues Miranda, Allan Cezar de Azevedo Martins, Clarissa Boschiero, Wanderley Rodrigues Bastos and Rosane Silva, ‘Contrasting the Microbiomes from Forest Rhizosphere and Deeper Bulk Soil from an Amazon Rainforest Reserve’, ScienceDirect, 15 November 2017, accessed on 2 July 2023, https://www.sciencedirect.com/science/article/abs/pii/S0378111917310065

digest sugars found in mother's milk. It helps control our blood sugar and cholesterol levels and is involved in almost every process of our body.

Since the microbiome is such an important part of our body, our health is highly dependent on the well-being and vibrancy of this diverse rainforest.

Even though the research results are still being debated, there is serious speculation that the bacteria in our gut could even be signalling our brain when we have eaten enough. These signals are thought to be sent from the gut to the brain by way of the vagus nerve. Experiments on animals have shown that when an animal is fully fed, a protein is released by the microbiome notifying the brain that the animal needs no more food and is satiated.

Mealtime brings a host of nutrients to our gut. Bacterial cells divide and multiply to replace microbes lost in stools. Some theorists have even philosophized that since gut microbes depend on their host for their own survival it is to their advantage if they remain a stable population and it would make sense if they had a way of communicating to the brain that they were satiated.

This is why calling the microbiome our second brain is not misplaced. However, life is complex and our microbiome can get quite unstable. It is constantly bombarded by pathogens that try to take it over. The real trouble starts when pathogens succeed.[84]

---

[84] 'The Microbiome', Harvard T. H. Chan, The Nutrition Source, accessed on 2 July 2023, https://www.hsph.harvard.edu/nutritionsource/microbiome

An unhealthy gut microbiome has been linked to a lot of diseases and conditions from diabetes, autism, stress to obesity. It has even been seen to affect the way certain drugs are assimilated and even affects our sleep patterns.

If you are to keep pathogens at bay, it is critical that you support your microbiome. A microbiome is supported by probiotics and good nutrients.

How to Maintain a Healthy Gut

A few simple steps may support the good microbes thereby strengthening them and giving them the wherewithal to defend against the pathogens. Indeed the benefits of a healthy gut include healthy weight, a stronger immune system and all the benefits that these two attributes bring with them like higher resistance to cardiovascular disease, diabetes and reduced blood pressure problems together with a host of related benefits.

It is clearly important that you nurture your microbiome with care and diligence. It has been overlooked for too long. Microbes in the gut have short lifespans and your microbiome is prone to changes fairly quickly since it is influenced by many factors like stress, exercise, sleep quality and sleep duration, antibiotics consumed, other medicines and diet. It is not only important to eat healthy, but also sleep well, exercise a bit and to keep stress under control. Simple additions to your meal will go a long way in building up a healthy microbiome. For example, eat fermented foods, like sauerkraut, pickles, kimchi and unprocessed yoghurt. You could add a probiotic to be taken daily for two months and cycle it every four months. Or eat vegetables high in fibre. Or make it a point to eat different foods even if in a mix of smal portions. No harm in you going around a buffet table with a colourfully filled plate. It will be good for your gut.

How to Lose Weight Without Losing Your Sanity

7

My Personal Experience at Weight Loss

Once I understood the dynamics of weight loss it was a breeze and I shed more than 27 kg without too much of a fuss. This chapter is not just about weight loss. It is relevant to you even if you are not looking to lose weight. It explains food dynamics and also how two hormones play a critical role not only in weight loss but also how they affect heart health, diabetes and a host of other avoidable sicknesses.

As a child my friends called me 'fatso' and even though they did not mean bad, I never felt good about it. It turned offensive when they called me 'Botato' the local slang for fat potato. But they were simply stating the fact. Is that all they saw in me? I was aghast and disheartened. I decided to get into shape. I tried and then took a break and stopped. Forgot about weight loss, I grew fatter, which made me try again. Life moved in a circle. Willpower was never my strength and I am not embarrassed to accept it. I often tried using it but as expected would draw a blank. In hindsight, I was actually using my weakness to surmount one of my life's biggest challenges. I had set myself up to fail. I had to find a different way forward. I had to get out of this mess and fortunately I was not the one to give up without a fight. I was trapped in my big body and simply could not get out of this mess. I was a reformed cigarette addict who went from more than a hundred cigarettes a day to zero without as much as a single withdrawal symptom worth its name. I had even learnt to live a happy life without them. I convinced myself that just as I walked away from the cigarette I was going to find a way out of this maze too. It took me many, many years and a lot of pain and 'humiliation' till I finally realized that weight loss was not that difficult after all. It was quite easy actually. Once the understanding that my health was my biggest asset and the resultant appreciation of how important it was sank in, I could no longer only wish to be healthy but started looking at ways and means of getting the situation under control. Weight loss was the only logical and obvious next step and this wish had to be followed up with action.

When I started with this my ultimate weight loss push I was the Goa club president of Skal International,[85] an international association of senior hospitality, travel and tourism industry professionals, the vice-chancellor of La Chaine des Rotisseurs,[86] a high-society foodie club and was also a prominent member of many other social clubs and associations. By profession I am a businessman who besides being a hotelier, coach and mentor also runs businesses manufacturing alcoholic beverages and importing and distributing high-end wines, spirits and beers. Thus, entertaining and being entertained is a routine. During this period, I was also elevated to be the national president for Skal International and then as its international councilor. I must confess though that even though I enjoyed being a member of the association, I left the Chaine des Rotisseurs since the delicious but high calorific meals were no longer in line with my new thinking. I did not leave it to stay away from temptation. I left the Chaine only because I had changed the way I saw food. This weight loss game can be easily won if you win over your mind.

My social engagements have not significantly changed and entertainment continues to play a major role in my life, yet I have almost effortlessly managed to shed more than 27 kg. Importantly, I have kept it away for many years now. Life for me has dramatically changed.

---

85 https://skal.org/home

86 https://www.chainedesrotisseurs.com/

'Success in life comes not from holding a good hand, but in playing a poor hand well.' Anonymous

I decided to pen down my thoughts which could help people like me understand that the road to good health, good looks and more importantly to an awesome feeling of success and happiness was not that tough and treacherous after all. I continued to meet friends, party hard and enjoy the better things of life. I did not deprive myself significantly. I decided to research on obesity and I realized that all I had to do was to take the same route that led me to success in giving up the cigarette. Only, this time I was looking for weight loss and good health.

Why People Find It So Hard to Lose Weight?

As I studied the various causes of obesity, I was shocked to realize that the food industry had actually been making a lot of money by playing with their labels and misguiding unsuspecting consumers like me. They were laughing their way to the bank while consumers like me were fighting a never-ending battle of the bulge. It is important to understand how this industry works because only then will you be able to see through the advertisements in media, and you will become a master at reading labels.

You will see how we had answers to the obesity conundrum many decades ago but it all got swept under the rug by business interests, economics and possibly even deliberate disinformation.

Why Do So Many People Suffer from Cardiovascular Disease, Hypertension And Diabetes?

As I have mentioned earlier, I have picked up data from the US due to easy availability of high-quality data.

Way back in 1977, the US Senate's Select Committee on Nutrition and Human Needs chaired by George McGovern [87] published what came to be known as the first comprehensive statement by the US government on the risk factors in the American diet. McGovern observed, 'Too much fat, too much sugar or salt, can be and are directly linked to heart disease, cancer, obesity and stroke.' Right through from 1970s to 2000, fat was continuously being made out to be the main culprit not only for coronary heart disease, but also for the obesity epidemic. This noise was getting louder with every passing year.

In 1988, the US surgeon general's report emphasized the health dangers of dietary fat. Twelve years later in 2000, the US government's 'Report on Nutrition and Health' stated fat was the unhealthiest part of the American diet.

No one factored in the social and economic factors that would influence the implementation of the anti-fat recommendations. What happened with the later reports

---

[87] Gerald M. Oppenheimer, I. Daniel Benrubi, 'McGovern's Senate Select Committee on Nutrition and Human Needs Versus the Meat Industry on the Diet–Heart Question (1976–1977)', National Library of Science, PubMed Central, January 2014, accessed on 2 July 2023, https://www.ncbi.nlm.nih.gov/pmc/articles/PMC3910043

was that all the focus went on fat control, and sugars and refined carbs, which were bigger culprits, were 'let off the hook'.

Simultaneously, behind closed doors the food industry magnates were very concerned with the repercussions the US government's dietary reports would have on the sales of their products. Packed food without fat can be quite tasteless and uninteresting. With time, however, they spotted enormous profits in this challenge. They suddenly realized that it was a huge opportunity. All they needed to do was to substitute fat with sugar.[88] The addition of sugar worked out so well that in the 1990s it led to a phenomenon called 'Snackwell Effect.[89] This refers to the tendency among dieters to over-consume low-calorie food in the belief that such food is healthier than high-calorie substitutes that cause them to gain weight. In reality, however, many dieters may be consuming a lot more calories during the day by overconsuming low-calorie food than they would if they simply stuck to a normal diet that includes high-calorific food.

Driven by consumer demand and an advertising blitzkrieg low-fat processed foods proliferated through

---

[88] P. K. Nguyen, S. Lin, P. Heidenreich, 'A Systematic Comparison of Sugar Content in Low-fat vs Regular Versions of Food', National Library of Medicine, PubMed Central, January 2016, accessed on 2 July 2023, https://www.ncbi.nlm.nih.gov/pmc/articles/PMC4742721

[89] 'What Is Snackwell Effect in Psychology?' *The Hindu*, 28 December 2018, https://www.thehindu.com/opinion/op-ed/what-is-snackwell-effect-psychology/article25842781.ece

grocery stores but unknown to most was that these were highly calorific and so were welcomed into millions of households by gullible weight watchers. To add to the confusion, the American Heart Association started labelling these low-fat foods with the heart symbol suggesting that these were healthy for the heart. They did not however label fresh foods as such, leaving the consumer confused and leaning towards packaged foods which carried the symbol. In the process, healthy food lost out to the packaged variety. By 1997, fifty-five companies participated in this labelling programme with over 600 products certified as 'healthy'. Many of these were cereal products like Kellogg's Frosted Flakes, Fruity Marshmallow Krispies and Low-Fat Pop Tarts.[90]

Around this time, a leading obesity researcher, Dr Jules Hirsch challenged the low-fat hypothesis. His studies suggested that when the fat content of a diet fell below 20 per cent, the body started producing saturated fat from carbohydrates. Another well-known researcher Dr Willett observed that substituting carbohydrates for fats could reduce the levels of high density lipoprotein (HDL) while raising triglycerides in the body. The former is sometimes called 'good' cholesterol. It was becoming clearer by the day that there were good fats and then there were bad fats. While the good fats were essential

[90] Ann F. La Berge, 'How the Ideology of Low Fat Conquered America', Oxford Academic, Journal of the History of Medicine and Allied Sciences, 23 February 2008, accessed on 2 July 2023, https://academic.oup.com/jhmas/article/63/2/139/772615

for heart health, Willet recommended that Americans give up the low fat diet and embrace good fats found in nuts and olive oil. Setting the cat among the pigeons, a later research also showed that dietary control could reduce cholesterol by 10 per cent since most of it is produced by our body. By now the average consumer was enjoying a delicious 'fat-free' diet but getting fatter with each bite. What many health gurus missed was that fat was not the *only* ingredient that affected good health and obesity in particular.

How We Brought This Obesity Epidemic on Ourselves

Now let us see what went wrong. You will see that we had the basic solutions to obesity years ago but either due to oversight or vested interests the truth was lost.

The Mediterranean diet with low-fat, less meat, more grains, vegetables, fruits and olive oil was promoted by Ancel Keys of the University of Minnesota, who discovered its health benefits.

On delving deeper, it became apparent to me that it was also very well known way back in the 1950s that innocent-looking eatables like bread, plain starchy foods, white rice and sweets lead to obesity. If we knew it all, how did we fail? Where did we go wrong?

America's most trusted name in child care and parenting, Benjamin Spock, made a similar observation in his bestselling book *Baby and Child Care* when it was first published in 1946.

Till about 1977, there was no official government advice regarding what was bad or good for obesity. It was the US Senate's Select Committee on Nutrition and Human Needs chaired by George McGovern that put the diet–heart hypothesis on its agenda. McGovern said, 'Too much fat, too much sugar or salt can be and are directly linked to heart disease, cancer, obesity and stroke.' The publication of this report led to the five-yearly publications of the US dietary guidelines. For the first time, Americans were told by their government what to eat. Fruits, vegetables, wholegrains, poultry and fish were on the recommended list while high-fat and high-sugar foods were to be reduced. These were great suggestions and if taken seriously should have resulted in a huge reduction in cardiovascular disease, diabetes and obesity.

This publication gave all the clarity needed and by now we should have all been healthy with obesity having been banished.

I hope by now you are beginning to understand where we went wrong and how we brought this obesity epidemic and various other health conditions upon us. If we can control obesity, we can control all the sicknesses that get exacerbated by it. Obesity is the root cause of many sicknesses. Too much fat, too much sugar or salt are directly linked to heart disease, cancer, obesity and stroke. It is no longer just about aesthetics.

For many years being obese was considered healthy and in some poorer societies in Asia and Africa it still is a sign of prosperity. Many studies have shown that obesity is primarily responsible for the diabetes epidemic, cardiovascular disease, hypertension, kidney problems and a host of other very serious conditions. If we could understand the cause of obesity, we could drastically reduce the damage brought about by the diseases caused by it.

It was Dr Atkins who argued that 'the low-fat approach to dieting promoted by the American Heart Association and others is creating an obesity epidemic'.[91]

Busting Obesity Myths

Having studied obesity in great depth I am happy to share with you certain other insights into the cause of the obesity epidemic. If you also understand these various aspects, you will be able to extrapolate and apply the same thinking to your individual wellness.

Please note: If you are looking out for weight loss or even diabetes control or even to implement some of the suggestions I have given below you must consult your doctor before using them as I am not a medical practitioner. I am delighted to share with you a very simple system which will help bring your weight and sugar problems under control and thus improve your overall health. This solution is based on hormones secreted by your body.

91 Ann F. La Berge, 'How the Ideology of Low Fat Conquered America', Oxford Academic, Journal of the History of Medicine and Allied Sciences, 23 February 2008, accessed on 25 February 2024, https://academic.oup.com/jhmas/article/63/2/139/772615

What I have shared below will give you a clear vision of the way forward.

Have you ever wondered:

- Why more than 90 per cent calorie-counting diets fail?
- Why most people who get into calorie-counting diets are soon back to their old obese selves? (Often such people are known to get even more obese on the rebound.)

Our body has no way of counting calories or for that matter keeping a balance between what we imbibe or utilize. For more than fifty years, we have been looking at obesity as the result of overeating or rather the excess of calories taken in versus those expended. While calories are important, there is much more to obesity control than just counting calories.

If our bodies could be brought back into shape just by counting calories, by the law of natural selection they should have been welcoming of low-calorie diets. It would not explain why more than 90 per cent of calorie-counting diets fail and most people who get into calorie-counting diets are soon back to their old obese selves. Often such people are known to get even more obese on the rebound.

Another misconception we have to deal with is that all calories are the same. To imagine that a load of calories from cookies would be digested the same way as the same number of calories from broccoli is absolutely ill-conceived. While calories may be important, the quality of food that we eat is equally important.

Most foods come as a combination of fats, carbs, proteins and fibre. Refined carbohydrates like bread and pastries are pure carbohydrates and just cannot be digested the same way as complex carbs like brown rice, wholewheat or so many vegetables.[92]

For too long we wrongly focused only on an energy-expenditure hypothesis of counting total calories. That cost us too many lives and a hell of a lot of money while also drastically cutting down our quality of life and as a result our longevity of living a good-quality life.[93]

At best we can take solace in the fact that we got it wrong; at worst we could surmise that we were deliberately misguided. Let us for a moment keep the calorie thermodynamics on the sidelines and take our focus on understanding the effect hormones have on our overall well-being.

Three Hormones That Affect Obesity

There are three major hormones that have a direct impact on obesity—insulin, glucagon and cortisol,

---

92 Claire Sissons, Medically reviewed by Katherine Marengo, 'What are Refined Carbohydrates?', MedicalNewsToday, 7 February 2020, accessed on 14 February 2024, https://www.medicalnewstoday.com/articles/refined-carbs#effects

93 Gary Taubes. *The Short Life and Weird Times of Cold Fusion*. Random House, 1993.

insulin being the big influencer. Without getting into the minutiae, proof justifying insulin hormonal effect can be easily found in the answers to the following questions.

Insulin

- If insulin is the cause of obesity, will its reduction make an obese person thin? [94]
- Can we make a thin person fat by giving them an excess of insulin?
- Could this one single change in thinking deliver to our Indian population relief from the prevalent diabetes epidemic?

The answer to these questions is yes. When insulin is prescribed to patients they generally gain weight. Patients with type 1 diabetes (which is shortage of insulin secretion by the pancreas) react to the shortage of insulin by losing weight.

Now that we know that insulin is an important contributor to obesity we need to focus on lowering it. Instead of focusing on reducing the main villain, we concentrate only on reducing the calories.

---

[94] Rashmi Ranjan Das, Manaswini Mangaraj, Saurav Nayak, Amit Kumar Satapathy, Samarendra Mahapatro and Jagdish Prasad Goyal, 'Prevalence of Insulin Resistance in Urban Indian School Children Who Are Overweight/Obese: A Cross-Sectional Study', National Library of Medicine, PubMed Central, Frontiers in Medicine, 12 February 2021, accessed 2 July 2023, https://www.ncbi.nlm.nih.gov/pmc/articles/PMC7907002

Thus, we need to regulate this powerful hormone called insulin. This can be easily done by reducing consumption of refined carbohydrates like pizza, white rice, etc., while simultaneously increasing the intake of complex carbs (lentils, chickpeas, etc.), proteins and fats.

In the light of this let me shoot down yet another often-touted diet programme. Some of us have been brought up to think that we need at least six small meals a day. We have been made to believe that it is healthy to eat a small meal every two hours a day. I cannot understand how this helps. There is not much research on its benefits either.

Glucagon

You could understand this from a different angle. Think of what happens when you sleep. When asleep or when fasting, sugar levels in the blood drop and so do the insulin levels. When insulin is down, it is a signal for glucagon to be released.[95] This results in glucagon stored in the liver being converted to glucose resulting in stored energy being released to keep our body energized. This energy is critical to keep our various organs, which do not sleep, energized and alive. If you can balance the two hormones, you will not gain weight.

---

95 James Norman, Medically Reviewed by Elena Christofides, 'What to Know About Insulin, Glucagon, and Regulation of Blood Glucose', Health Central, 24 January 2023, accessed on 2 July 2023, https://www.healthcentral.com/condition/type-1-diabetes/human-insulin-vs-analog

Cortisol

Cortisol is another hormone which plays an important role in promoting obesity.[96] It is our stress hormone. Unfortunately, the adrenal glands tend to secrete too much of it when we are stressed over a long period of time. In ancient times, humans were at a greater risk of being attacked by wild animals. The other main stressors were wars, floods and famines as these invariably resulted in a scarcity of food. During those primordial days, our body found a way to alert us when it sensed we were in danger of being attacked or when there was a likelihood of starvation to death. Put plainly, we were designed to feel stress when danger was near.

Our 'body model' has hardly changed in the last 60,000 years. No sooner we feel stress, it releases cortisol which messages every cell of our body to slow down its metabolic rate to conserve energy in the form of fat as body fuel for future use.

Today an abundance of food is available in most of the civilized world and common chronic stress comes from jobs, relationships, financial concerns, health, etc., while in the past stress used to be in passing phases. In our modern world, many remain under stress continuously for a major part of their lives. Our body when under stress

---

96 S. D. Hewagalamulage, T. K. Lee, I. J. Clarke, B. A. Henry, 'Stress, Cortisol, and Obesity: A Role for Cortisol Responsiveness in Identifying Individuals Prone to Obesity', National Library of Medicine, PubMed, 31 March 2016, accessed on 7 July 2023, https://pubmed.ncbi.nlm.nih.gov/27345309

still commands cells to lower their metabolic rate so as to stock up on energy for the future.

Stress control is often an ignored tool in weight management. But it can really hit you in the waist.

We will always have imperfections to live with. However, if you are overweight and have this urge to lose weight do not wait till tomorrow. The right time to shed pounds is when you wake up to the reality that you are obese and are ready to take the trouble to change the situation. That time could be in the middle of the Christmas or Diwali festivities or it could be during a fasting period. It is often after Diwali or the new year that most of us become conscious of the thick flab around our waist.

I repeat, there is no good time to start. If you do not start early, you could miss on the opportunity. The problem with losing such an opening is that you may not die nor get a heart attack as a result but *may not be far from one*. We all would like to live normal healthy lives.

You could have a healthy life ahead if only you will take the time to focus on the fundamentals that I have explained throughout this book.

Once you know which foods are bad for you, once you know you can party and enjoy life and yet eat what you feel like not because you *need* to but because you *want* to, why do you need willpower? Do you need willpower to tell you that your body feels a bit of a tremble after having too much of caffeine? You know how it feels and so you avoid too much of it. You will stick to your limits—whatever those are. You just need to become aware of your body's limits. Learn to listen to it. I have suggestions on this later in the book. Once you listen to your body, you will hear it saying '*Stop*' and you will automatically stop eating. You will no longer need your willpower to stop eating. You need to develop the power to listen.

This is the only body you will ever have—nurture it and see the wonders it will do for you.

I once asked a centenarian for the secret to longevity. He said, 'It is very simple. I have no grudges, no hatred, no resentment. Every day when I open my eyes, I say, "This is the day the Lord has made. Let me rejoice."

'The secret of life is good health which helps us feel joy and happiness and then we have inner peace. The only being that can laugh is the human being. It is the finest way in the world to release tension. So laugh and enjoy the present moment.'

Busting Myths about Diets and Disease

8

The Devil Is in the Sugar—Exorcise It

Sugar not only makes you fat, but also sick.[97] For a better understanding, imagine the following scenario.

You have just had a wonderfully tasty meal and are easing into a quick nap. What you cannot see is the work going on 'behind the scenes' in your belly. A very important organ that immediately goes into action is

[97] James M. Rippe and Theodore J. Angelopoulos, 'Relationship between Added Sugars Consumption and Chronic Disease Risk Factors: Current Understanding', National Library of Medicine, PubMed Central, 4 November 2016, accessed on 7 July 2023, https://www.ncbi.nlm.nih.gov/pmc/articles/PMC5133084

your liver. The liver as we know it was developed at least 400,000 years ago. You are reading right, our liver as we know it today was developed 4,000 centuries ago and it is just the same since then. It does the work of a metabolic supercomputer. Unfortunately, this supercomputer is incapable of processing refined sugar and processed foods.

When we overload this computer, it slows down and with time we expose ourselves to diseases.

Let us take a look at what we eat:

Today an average person consumes about 300 gm of sugar daily. If you do not believe me, look up all the labels of all the processed foods that you buy. Add to that the sodas that you pop, and you are highly likely to cross 300 gm. If you do not consume a lot of sugar, consider yourself blessed.

All we eat can broadly be broken down into carbohydrate, fat, protein and fibre.[98]

Carbohydrate gets converted into→ Sugar
Fat gets converted into→ Fatty acids and glycerol
Protein gets converted into→ Amino acids
Fibre gets converted into→Cellulose

The sugar gets broken down into approximately 80 per cent glucose and the balance mostly into fructose.

[98] USDA, National Agriculture Library, https://www.nal.usda.gov/human-nutrition-and-food-safety/food-composition/macronutrients

In India and indeed around the world, we are going through an epidemic of sicknesses far worse than the Covid-19 pandemic. The same was not true five decades ago. The deaths are many times greater in number but what is worse is that we seem to think they are natural and normal so have stopped even looking out for an urgent solution.

The Obesity Epidemic: A Study

Most of us weigh at least 10 kg more than our ideal weight. This is not an exaggeration and I am not even referring to the seriously obese ones .

What do the Mediterranean diet, the Atkins diet, the Palaeo diet and the Japanese diet all have in common?

They all eliminate fructose because they accept that it is as bad as cyanide.

My research into the longevity of life compels me to ask the following questions:

- How come there were not so many fat people around the world in the 1960s?
- How come there were not so many diabetics in the 1960s? Is it just a coincidence that the number of obese and the number of diabetics increased almost simultaneously since then?
- How come only a few decades ago India was known for its starving millions but now has its

millions of obese persons? [99]

In a quiet little room, just like millions of Indian boys and girls, Aryan lay in his bed while a small unit above the window blasts chilled air. Outside, the temperature in Mumbai was a scorching 41°C.

These days, even middle-class families in India can afford air conditioning, but this was not that way in the early 1970s when I was growing up.

Since most of the time, our house was dark and hot due to frequent power failure, as soon as the sun began its descent, I would run outside to play with my siblings, neighbours and friends. I liked football, which can be physically exhausting especially during the hot weather.

Aryan tells me that kids do not do that anymore.

'Why would we when we have the comfort of air conditioning and also data on our mobiles?'

He asked that with a look of disgust.

At 96 kg, Aryan is obese. And seems to be getting fatter by the day just like the majority of our population.

Many of us struggle with weight not only due to our sedentary lifestyle, but also due to a new-found love for unhealthy food that is easily affordable with our growing economic 'power'. We now eat out quite frequently something which we older ones never did in our youth. Back then, snacking meant buying cheap Indian street food, which usually came in small portions and was made fresh.

[99] Geeta Pandey, 'Childhood Obesity: Why are Indian Children Getting Fatter?', BBC News, Delhi, 29 July 2022, accessed on 7 July 2023, https://www.bbc.com/news/world-asia-india-62307784

The idea that Indians have a weight problem is difficult for me to digest because India was notorious for its high malnutrition rates—higher than even sub-Saharan Africa.[100] We are a country where obesity has skyrocketed into a national crisis and on the other side of the spectrum we still have millions who are undernourished. Like some of India's other problems, obesity partly stems from the country leapfrogging generations in industrial development. American industrialization took more than a century; India is trying to catch up within a few decades.

To put things into perspective, from 2014 to 2018 there has been an increase of 86.7 per cent bariatric surgeries taking the number from around 11,000 in 2014 to more than 20,000 in 2018.[101]

---

100 Swaroop Kumar Sahu, S. Ganesh Kumar, B. Vishnu Bhat, K.C. Premarajan, Sonali Sarkar, Gautam Roy and Nitin Joseph, 'Malnutrition among Under-five children in India and Strategies for Control', National Library of Medicine, PubMed Central, Journal of Natural Science, Biology and Medicine, January 2015, accessed on 14 January 2024,https://www.ncbi.nlm.nih.gov/pmc/articles/PMC4367032

101 Aparna Govil Bhasker, Arun Prasad, P. Praveen Raj, Randeep Wadhawan, Manish Khaitan, Abhay Jugal Agrawal, Om Tantia, Sarfaraz J. Baig, Raj Palaniappan, H. V. Shivaram, Sumeet Shah, Vandana Soni, Mohit Bhandari, Rakesh Shivhare, Shrihari Dhorepatil, Pradeep Chowbey, Mahendra Narwaria, Shashank Shah, Rajesh Khullar, 'Obesity and Metabolic Surgery Society of India', https://pubmed.ncbi.nlm.nih.gov/32333322/#:~:text=Trends%20and%20progress%20of%20bariatric%20and%20metabolic%20surgery%20in%20India', National Library of Medicine, PubMed Central, 24 April 2020, accessed on 7 July 2023, https://pubmed.ncbi.nlm.nih.gov/32333322

Obesity has led to a host of other health woes growing at an alarming rate in India, including hypertension and diabetes.[102]

If we look at how widespread obesity is in India, we could soon be the world's fattest nation.

All this could not have been caused by a mutation in our genes since none was recorded. Was it that our environment had changed? I could smell something at the end of the dark tunnel. If it was our environment, what in it changed so drastically that affected disparate populations, not only in India, but across the world? As if lit up by a very powerful torchlight suddenly the main suspect became obvious. It was clear that the culprit was none other than our dear and sometimes most beloved friend called sugar. Read on and you will understand why sugar.

We have been brought up to think that if we managed the calories consumed and made them equal to calories spent all would be well. The logic in this case being 'If you ate it you'd better burn it or it would accumulate in your gut as fat until you found it possible to burn it'. It implied that you could eat anything you wanted as long as you would burn it all up. I used to believe this and maybe you believe this even until now but give yourself some time to understand and you too will know the truth. This assumption is absolutely wrong.

102 'Abdominal Obesity in India: Analysis of the National Family Health Survey-5 (2019–2021) Data', The Lancet Regional health, South East Asia,12 May 2023, accessed on 7 July 2023, https://www.thelancet.com/journals/lansea/home

No one chooses to be fat. The obese are victims. This stuff called fat creeps into them without even their knowledge. By the time they realize what is going on, they could be 20 kgs overweight. There are innumerable people trying their best to lose weight but simply cannot. They just go on binging despite wanting to stop and then feel terribly guilty later. What could be the matter? Why can't their stomachs signal to their brain that they have had enough and need to stop? Can you explain to me why children below the age of seven should be obese? Never was it known to be this bad. What has changed? If we are talking about the obese not getting enough exercise, you need to explain to me how there are so many obese babies.

Let us get into the dynamics of it all. We are surely eating more today than thirty years ago. *Why*? Food was there even then. No one really ate all that much and grew this fat. Look at the wild. Even the lion will not look at a meal after he is satiated.

How come humans have a problem? This brings me to a fourth hormone we do not really hear too much of. There is a control system in our abdomen set up by the hormone leptin which sends a signal to the brain to stop eating. It sends a signal of satiety. If we are eating much more today than we were before it is probably because leptin is not doing its job. If it were working normally, we will be in a position to produce and burn energy in such amounts that keep our body happy, energized and healthy. At this point, we are in a state of homeostasis. Recent studies show that over the last thirty-year period, we are eating at least 250 calories more per day. So, what went wrong with this robust and dynamic signalling system that worked so well for human species for more than a million years? What came in the way of this system of fat control and disturbed its working resulting in such a huge energy imbalance? Is there something in our system that is blocking us from maintaining an equilibrium between calories consumed versus calories burned?

> ***'No one chooses to be fat. The obese are victims.'***

How come the lion will let a lamb walk by unharmed when it is full but we frequently overeat? It is none other than leptin resistance.[103]

When the American Heart Association, the USDA and the American Medical Association all directed the American citizens to cut down on the consumption of fats (the world soon followed), the food industry substituted fats with carbohydrates in order to maintain taste in food.[104] This they expected would drastically cut

---

103 Alexandra Shapiro, Nihal Tümer, Yongxin Gao, Kit-Yan Cheng and Philip J. Scarpace, 'Prevention and Reversal of Diet-induced Leptin Resistance with a Sugar-free Diet Despite High Fat Content', Cambridge University Press, Cambridge Core, 22 March 2011, accessed on 8 July 2023, https://www.cambridge.org/core/journals/british-journal-of-nutrition/article/prevention-and-reversal-of-dietinduced-leptin-resistance-with-a-sugarfree-diet-despite-high-fat-content/B5151988E8E23EB1F7CC75565B2BE069

104 Ian Leslie, 'The Sugar Conspiracy', *The Guardian*, 7 April 2016, accessed on 8 July 2023, https://www.theguardian.com/society/2016/apr/07/the-sugar-conspiracy-robert-lustig-john-yudkin

the incidence of cardiovascular disease that was getting difficult to manage. It resulted in a boom of the fat-free business. Shelves in supermarkets were full of fat-free cakes, chocolates, cookies, etc.

If that was the best way to go, we should have had much lower rates of heart disease. But that did not happen. On the contrary, sicknesses increased drastically along with obesity and type 2 diabetes. So who was the culprit? Was it the carbohydrates that substituted the fat that was removed from our diet? If yes, which were these naughty carbohydrates? It was no coincidence that around the same time, the price of high fructose corn syrup dropped drastically and sugar not only became increasingly affordable to the less affluent, but also to the beverage companies which could now use it liberally.[105] If you go back to the consumption pattern studies done during this same period you will find a huge increase in the consumption of soft drinks.[106] With regard to a cola, the calculation is pretty straightforward. The law of thermodynamics states that if you consume 3,500 calories and do not burn it, you add about half a kilo fat.

---

[105] Harvard T.H. Chan, School of Public Health, News, 'Have Low-fat Diets Made Us Fatter?', accessed on 14 January 2024, https://www.hsph.harvard.edu/news/hsph-in-the-news/have-low-fat-diets-made-us-fatter/

[106] Vasanti S. Malik, Matthias B. Schulze and Frank B. Hu, 'Intake of Sugar-sweetened Beverages and Weight Gain: A Systematic Review', National Library of Science, PubMed Central, 8 November 2011, accessed on 9 July 2023, https://www.ncbi.nlm.nih.gov/pmc/articles/PMC3210834

A small can of cola gives at least 150 calories. Drunk daily for a year totals 54,750 avoidable calories. This would result in a weight gain of 7 kg.

The Culprit: High-Fructose Corn Syrup

Why don't we stop eating when the total calories consumed from the soft drinks and food have crossed what should be our average calorie intake? Shouldn't we be feeling full? Why leptin does not kick in when we are satiated? Why does this control mechanism not stop us from overeating? Imagine the mess and destruction if the rail signalling system went awry at a train intersection.

Till now, I am only counting calories from a small bottle of cola. Let us now talk about the bigger ones which are commonly sold. So, are soft drinks the cause of obesity? It depends on whom you ask. Many so-called health experts funded by the soft drink associations will surely tell you that the drinks are only dangerous if consumed in excess. If you ask independent researchers, they will confirm that the main culprit in the obesity epidemic is the soft drink followed rather closely by the packed 'fresh' fruit juices.

So the next logical question is: What is there in soft drinks that confuses our signalling system? Is it the added sodium or the sugar?[107] We all know that the

[107] Gill Shaffer, 'Sugar vs Salt: Which Is Worse for Your Heart Health?', Future You Cambridge, 21 February 2020, accessed on 9 July 2023, https://futureyouhealth.com/knowledge-centre/sugar-vs-salt

amount of sodium in these beverages is minuscule, so the culprit has to be sugar. High-fructose corn syrup (HFCS) is commonly used in the soft drink industry as a sweetener. Currently, through beverages and processed foods, many of us consume about 35 kg of HFCS a year. This is approximately 100 gm per day. That is assuming that all consume 35 kg. If one were to remove from the study those who hardly had any processed foods or soft drinks, the quantity of sugar consumed remain practically the same and the figure per individual would shoot up drastically. HFCS is used by the industry because it is not only sweeter than table sugar but also cheaper. It helps the conglomerates make huge profits. Who cares if it is at the cost of the common gullible citizen? Is this only a discussion about calories and how to reduce them? No, it is a discussion about how bad fructose is and how it damages leptin's alerting system that our bodies have been accustomed to for millions of years. Fructose is a part of table sugar but forms an even greater portion of the HFCS.

Going down memory lane, we would only get our fructose from fruits and vegetables. If we totalled all that we consumed, it would not really be very significant. The beverage industry was not using too much of it then. The problem started when the processed food industry and the beverage industry honed in on the inexpensive HFCS to replace fat.

Why am I discussing so much about fructose and not sugar as a whole? It is because of the fructose component of sugar. The liver treats fructose differently from glucose, which we also get in sugar. Fructose does not suppress the hunger hormone ghrelin and also interferes with leptin's satiety signals to the brain. This is why even if you have had a jug full of cola and the accompanying ton of calories you do not have a problem eating a heavy meal soon after. This is because leptin does not send out a satiety signal and since the hunger hormone is not suppressed, it keeps signalling hunger to the brain.

Unlike glucose, fructose does not even stimulate the production of insulin so leptin does not go up. If leptin does not rise, a signal cannot be sent to the brain to say that one needs to stop eating. Seen from this angle, we are beset with two major problems and both these are caused by the fructose in sugar. First, since ghrelin is not suppressed it keeps signalling hunger to our brain and this is justified since leptin is also not produced to signal to the brain that we are satiated.[108] High ingestion of fructose is also known to cause obesity, lipid problems, hypertension, and type 2 diabetes and cardiovascular disease.[109] It affects

---

108 Karen L. Teff, Sharon S. Elliott, Matthias Tschöp, Timothy J. Kieffer, Daniel Rader, Mark Heiman, Raymond R. Townsend, Nancy L. Keim, David D'Alessio, Peter J. Havel, 'Dietary Fructose Reduces Circulating Insulin and Leptin, Attenuates Postprandial Suppression of Ghrelin, and Increases Triglycerides in Women', Oxford Academic, *The Journal of Clinical Endocrinology & Metabolism*, 1 June 2004, accessed on 9 July 2023, https://academic.oup.com/jcem/article/89/6/2963/2870348

109 Sarah A Hannou, Danielle E Haslam, Nicola M. McKeown and Mark A Herman, 'Fructose Metabolism and Metabolic Disease', National Library of Science, PubMed, 1 February 2018, accessed on 9 July 2023, https://pubmed.ncbi.nlm.nih.gov/29388924

the liver which finds it difficult to handle. The synthesis of fructose in the liver is known to result in gout which is hugely related to hypertension, which is also getting endemic.[110]

Glucose on the other hand is processed most easily by the liver. Studies have shown that when one consumes an equal quantity of glucose and fructose while most of the glucose gets assimilated into the body and through the liver into glycogen and energy, at least 30 per cent of fructose gets stored as fat in the body.[111] So, is fructose fatty? It could just as well be called fat.

By implication, is sugar poisonous?[112] Given that it is causing the metabolic syndrome epidemic (obesity, hypertension, cardiovascular disease, type 2 diabetes and other lipid problems), it should be avoided. Recent

---

[110] Liji Thomas, Reviewed by Chloe Barnett, 'Why Does Added Sugar Influence Gout?', News Medical Life Sciences, accessed on 9 July 2023, https://www.news-medical.net/health/Why-Does-Added-Sugar-Influence-Gout.aspx

[111] Justin S. Rhodes, 'Research shows fructose increases body fat and decreases physical activity', Beckman Institute, 1 June 2015, accessed on 9 July 2023,https://beckman.illinois.edu/about/news/article/2015/06/01/194d2053-38d3-4949-b30a-7dc5b16acdd7#:~:text=Research%20in%20Justin%20Rhodes'%20laboratory,inactivity%2C%20and%20body%20fat%20deposition

[112] 'The Sweet Danger of Sugar', Harvard Health Publishing, Harvard Medical School, Heart Health, 9 January 2022, accessed on 9 July 2023, https://www.health.harvard.edu/heart-health/the-sweet-danger-of-sugar#:~:text=Over%20time%2C%2Cthis%20can%20lead,pathological%20pathways%20to%20heart%20disease

studies have also proven that the earlier children are exposed to heavy consumption of sugar, the more likely they will crave it later. Studies show that newborns have a predisposition to eat a lot of sugar if their mothers' consume a lot of it during pregnancy.[113]

When you talk of high-fat diets doing bad things, you should also be referring to high-fructose diets doing the same. Also, low-fat diets do not work when the low fat is substituted by carbohydrates containing sugars, which result in high fat accumulation.

If You Remain Blind to Diabetes, It Could Make You Blind

Continuing with our sugar story, we cannot talk about longevity of life without tackling diabetes. It is one of the world's top killers. I believe it is a true serial killer because a lot of research points to the fact that diabetes could be responsible for cardiovascular disease, stroke, Alzheimer's and even cancer. The killer does not kill instantly but eats away at the core of our being. Think of white ants eating away a grand piano which looks solid and sturdy on the

---

113 M.I. Goran, J.F. Plows, E.E. Ventura, 'Effects of Consuming Sugars and Alternative Sweeteners during Pregnancy on Maternal and Child Health: Evidence for a Second-hand Sugar Effect', National Library of Medicine, PubMed, HHS Public Access, 3 December 2018, accessed on 14 January 2024, https://www.ncbi.nlm.nih.gov/pmc/articles/PMC7441786/#:~:text=Even%20before%20birth%2C%20fetuses%20can,influence%20offspring%20growth%20and%20development

outside while going hollow from within. Diabetes mellitus is a disease which disturbs our body's ability to fully utilize the energy it receives from food. Broadly speaking, there are two types of diabetes.[114]

1. In Type 1 diabetes, the pancreas cannot produce adequate quantities of insulin that is required to carry sugar from the blood into the cells to be utilized for energy.
2. In Type 2 diabetes, the pancreas secretes adequate quantities of insulin but the cells are resistant to it and so greater quantities of insulin need to be produced to deliver sugar into the cells. The pancreas is put under pressure as the resistance increases with time and more and more insulin is required to carry the same quantity of sugar across the cell wall. This condition is called insulin resistance.

The following explanation will help you understand in a very simplistic manner what diabetes is all about.

When we eat or drink, most of our food is broken down into a simple sugar called glucose. Glucose provides the energy our body needs for its daily activities.

Blood vessels and blood are the highways that transport sugar to the cells where it is used in muscles or where it is stored in the form of fat. Sugar cannot

114 'Diabetes', Cleveland Clinic, last reviewed 17 February 2023, accessed on 9 July 2023, https://my.clevelandclinic.org/health/diseases/7104-diabetes

cross the cell walls on its own. The hormone insulin plays the role of the key that opens the way for sugar to pass through the cell walls to be then used for energy. When sugar moves out of the bloodstream into the cells, the blood sugar level is lowered. If there is no insulin to carry the sugar out of the blood and into the cells, it causes the blood sugar to rise. Too much sugar in the blood is called hyperglycemia or high blood sugar.

What Causes Diabetes?

The causes of diabetes are not very clear but the following factors seem to play a significant role:[115]

- Genes
- Diet
- Obesity
- Physical stress such as surgery or illness
- Use of certain medications like steroids
- A poorly functioning pancreas
- High blood pressure
- High blood cholesterol or triglyceride levels
- Old age
- Smoking

Symptoms of diabetes include:[116]

115 'Diabetes Risk Factors', American Heart Association, last reviewed 5 May 2021, accessed on 9 July 2023, https://www.heart.org/en/health-topics/diabetes/understand-your-risk-for-diabetes

116 'Symptoms, Diagnosis and Monitoring of Diabetes', American Heart Association, Heart Attack and Stroke Symptoms, last reviewed 5

- Increased thirst
- Increased hunger (especially after eating)
- Dry mouth
- Frequent urination
- Unexplained weight loss (even though you are eating normally)
- Slow-healing sores or cuts

Symptoms of low blood sugar or hypoglycemia are seen when blood sugar is less than 70 mg/dl. When blood sugar is low, one's body gives out signals that it needs food. Different people have different symptoms.

Common symptoms of low blood sugar include:

- Feeling weak
- Feeling dizzy
- Feeling hungry
- Pounding heart
- Feeling frightened or anxious
- Feeling confused
- Headache
- Poor coordination
- Having frequent nightmares
- Difficulty to focus
- Passing out

May 2021, accessed on 9 July 2023, https://www.heart.org/en/health-topics/diabetes/symptoms-diagnosis--monitoring-of-diabetes

How to Prevent Diabetes[117]

There are many ways to prevent the dreaded disease. Keeping one's weight in check, staying active and eating a healthy diet (a healthy diet can be very tasty too) can keep this dreaded disease at bay.

A diet rich in wholegrains and healthy fats helps. Mono-and polysaturated fats help lower risk of diabetes and heart disease. Canola and olive oil are great choices. Avocados, nuts and seeds are great supports to good health.

The devil is in the refined grains and sugary sodas. Stay away from them at all costs. White bread, white rice, pasta and potatoes cause spikes in blood sugar. Sugary soft drinks, fruit punch and artificial fruit juice also have a similar effect on blood sugar. To lower your risk, switch to wholegrains and skip sugary drinks.

A Closer Look at Sugar

Till the late 1800s, sugar was a luxury afforded only by the rich. Indeed, it was a status symbol. It was only when sugar production became mechanized that its supply increased dramatically and as a result its price dropped drastically, which made it affordable. For the middle and lower classes, sugar consumption symbolized economic

117 Mayo Clinic Staff, 'Diabetes Prevention: 5 Tips for Taking Control', Mayo Clinic, 24 March 2023, accessed on 9 July 2023, https://www.mayoclinic.org/diseases-conditions/type-2-diabetes/in-depth/diabetes-prevention/art-20047639

freedom and implied raising their social status. So what is wrong with sugar?

Consumption of Sugar Is Directly Linked to Weight Gain

Sugar is important as our body generates energy from it, but the sugar our body utilizes is not the one commonly consumed by us in our tea or coffee and soda. A minuscule part of this sugar is used up for energy while a lot of it gets put away as fat and results in weight gain and obesity. This weight gain brings along with it major sicknesses like type 2 diabetes, cardiovascular disease. This is not a scientific journal, so I will not get into the details of how sugar creates type 2 diabetes, but the research is all there for you to read should you want to verify my observation. There is a never-ending debate that sugar could even be addictive,[118] which could explain why even though we all know that sugar is bad we continue consuming it.

[118] Anna Schaefer and Kareem Yasin, Medically reviewed by Miho Hatanaka, 'Experts Agree: Sugar Might Be as Addictive as Cocaine', Healthline, updated on 30 May 2023, accessed on 9 July 2023, https://www.healthline.com/health/food-nutrition/experts-is-sugar-addictive-drug

Sugar Ups Your Blood Pressure And Heart Disease Risk[119]

Studies have proven that sugar also contributes to high cholesterol and cardiovascular disease. High intake of sugar also increases blood pressure.

Think of it, your heart pumps from the time you are in your mother's womb till the day you die. It pumps approximately 200 million litres across a lifetime. If you are not impressed by this figure, look at it differently. During your lifetime your heart pumps 10,000 tankers of 20,000 litres of blood each. To make it even simpler, your heart pumps approximately 125 tankers every year. How can any person put obstacles in the path of this most important pump?

Sugar Messes with Your Brain's Signals[120]

It is widely accepted that sugar being addictive has an effect on the brain. By regularly consuming sugar, we condition our brain to seek out sweet-tasting foods and this leads to increased consumption.

---

119 'Know Your Risk for Heart Disease', Centers for Disease Control and Prevention, Heart Disease, last reviewed on 21 March 2023, accessed on 9 July 2023, https://www.cdc.gov/heartdisease/risk_factors.htm

120 Ferris Jabr, 'How Sugar and Fat Trick the Brain into Wanting More Food', Neuroscience, 1 January 2016, accessed on 9 July 2023, https://www.scientificamerican.com/article/how-sugar-and-fat-trick-the-brain-into-wanting-more-food

Sugar Almost Never Leaves You Feeling Full

Sugar does not supress ghrelin. Sugar delivers to you a load of empty calories, which do not make you feel full. Calories that you consume from sugary drinks are not even counted since your body is used to overlooking them when eating meals. This results in double calorie intake.

Sugar Slows Down Your Brain[121]

Sugar is your brain's big enemy. It is now known that it not only causes blood sugar and blood pressure, but also quickens the onset of brain atrophy resulting in dementia and Alzheimer's.

Sugar Rots Your Teeth

Just as you love sugar, so do the millions of oral bacteria residing within you. When they feast on it, they release certain acids that erode the enamel off your teeth that help them penetrate even deeper into your teeth leaving the sparkling white little things looking all black and spoilt. Add to that, the cavities that become fermentation vessels giving out bad breath.

Cutting down on sugar alone will add many high-quality years to your life and it is not even a difficult thing to do.

---

[121] Ibid.

The Biggest Obstacle to Letting Go of Sugar—You

I have known many people who have decided to let go of sugar. Some of them even pat themselves for not consuming it whatsoever but hardly do they know that sugar sneaks into their body unknowingly!

Below, I have compiled a few pointers that will throw light on how we are all susceptible to being tricked by this great trickster called sugar.

Added sweeteners are infused in processed food in gargantuan ways that will shock you. Almost all packed foods have added sugars called by different and often deceptive names.

Once you become aware that sugar does you no good but on the contrary works on your body like poison, it becomes obvious that you strategize to at least reduce your consumption of it. I will not say 'giving up sugar' as it would imply a sacrifice. However, you cannot be sacrificing when you know that you are just correcting a wrong that will make your body healthy. You will not feel as if you are depriving yourself of a goodie, as that will make giving up all the more difficult.

Let us call it 'letting go of sugar'. Trust me, it is entirely possible to eat less sugar without any sacrifice whatsoever. I am reminded of how I stopped mixing sugar and milk in my coffee. I did not miss a thing. On the contrary, I can now taste the coffee for what it is rather than consuming a mix that is not the real thing in the first place. I can now sniff at the floral, spicy, fruity and earthy coffee fragrance while savouring the strong buttery, bitter and burnt taste of rich coffee between my lips.

Let me walk you through simple systems that will enable you to make smart food choices thereby reducing your sugar consumption while still keeping the sweetness of your life intact albeit with a lot less sugar.

Tea, coffee and desserts form just the tip of the iceberg. The dilemma is that sugar is now all-pervasive. It is ubiquitous and yet hidden. It is so prevalent that one needs a strategy to avoid it. Sugar is so deceptive that in many cases you will not find it even though it is often omnipresent. Once there is a strategy to locate it, it becomes easy to objectively decide what to eat and what not to.

Where Can We Find This Hidden Sugar?

I was speaking to a staff of a well-known fast-food chain and was stunned when he candidly mentioned that sugar was added to almost everything they made. This included bread, burger, tomato sauce and even mustard sauce. Did you know that every squirt of tomato sauce pours out almost one teaspoon of dissolved sugar?

How many people have told you to eat flavoured yogurt as a healthy breakfast food? Each of these little innocent-looking yogurt cups are laden with teaspoons of sugar.

We are surrounded by such sugar-spiked foods and we do not even know it. The most important step to counter this and take control of our lives is to build an awareness of how we get fooled.

A Few Myths And Truths about Sugar And Its Friends

Honey, Is It Good for You?

If I have diabetes can I substitute sugar with honey?[122]

Unlike the common perception, there is hardly any difference between sugar and honey. The two would be just about the same if one left out the vitamins and antioxidants that come with the honey but are absent in refined sugar. Honey metabolizes in much the same way as sugar and contains about the same quantity of fructose as sugar. I recommend we do not muddle ourselves and stay away from honey, corn syrup, maple syrup as these are all very deceptive sugar substitutes. Here is a list of the various names of sugar.

[122] M. Regina Castro, 'Diabetes foods: Can I substitute honey for sugar?', Mayo Clinic, 8 July 2023, accessed on 9 July 2023, https://www.mayoclinic.org/diseases-conditions/diabetes/expert-answers/diabetes/faq-20058487

Sixty-five Alternative Names of Sugar

Barley malt	Castor sugar	Lactose	Malt	Rice syrup
Barbados sugar	Date sugar	Maltose	Maltodextrin	Sorbitol
Evaporated cane juice	Dehydrated cane juice	High fructose corn syrup or HFCS	Fruit juice concentrate	Free flowing brown sugars
Brown sugar	Demerara sugar	Glucose	Malt syrup	Sucrose
Buttered syrup	Dextran	Glucose solids	Marnitol	Granulated sugar
Cane juice	Dextrose	Golden sugar	Maple syrup	Treacle
Cane sugar	Diastatic malt	Golden syrup	Molasses	Turbinado sugar
Caramel	Diastase	Grape sugar	Muscovado	Yellow sugar
Corn syrup	Ethyl maltol	Galactose	Panccha	Agave nectar
Corn syrup solids	Sorghum syrup	Honey	Powdered sugar	Cane crystals
Confectioner's sugar	Fructose	Icing sugar	Raw sugar	Corn sweetener
Carob syrup	Fruit juice	Invert sugar	Refiner's syrup	Crystalline fructose
Beet sugar	Syrup	Starch	Table sugar	Maltotroise

Source: The Health Sciences Academy, '65 Alternative Names of Sugar', accessed on 26 February 2024, https://thehealthsciencesacademy.org/wp-content/uploads/2014/08/The-Health-Sciences-Academy_65-Names-Of-Sugar.pdf

What about Fruits?

Eating fruits is a good idea because they are not only rich in vitamins, iron, antioxidants and natural sugar, but also gives you the much needed fibre. Sugar, when we have in the form of fruit, takes time to breakdown and so allows time for the liver to function optimally. Drinking fruit juice[123] however is not a good idea as it delivers sugar straight to the liver.

---

[123] Cleveland Clinic Staff, 'Is 100% Fruit Juice Good for You?' , Cleveland Clinic, Health Essentials, Nutrition, 25 October 2022, accessed on 9 July 2023,https://health.clevelandclinic.org/is-100-percent-fruit-juice-as-healthy-as-it-sounds

If you must have fruit juice, keep your portions small. Even though they may not have added sugars, their efficient sugar delivery system makes them dangerous.

Processed Foods, Are They Really Bad?

These are the main problem areas. You will need to do away with as many of these suspects as possible for about a month. After that you could add some of them back one at a time as you desire. By doing this, you would have eliminated quite a large percentage of these disrupter foods.

What about Sodas?

They are bad. Stay away from them

Is Cereal for Breakfast a Good Idea?

I recommend two possible strategies for breakfast not to become your morning dessert. Move away from packed foods and cereals. Most packed foods and cereals come with added sugar in some form or the other. The best strategy would be to eat home-made eggs, plain yogurt and fruits for breakfast.

What about Snacks?

Do not indulge in snacking. Give your stomach a break as it also needs to rest. Snacks like energy bars or dried fruit are highly deceptive and may be bracketed together with desserts, which are avoidable. If you are going to have any of these and think you are 'being good', you would be bluffing yourself.

If you have to snack, have a few tree nuts; even popcorn without any toppings will do but keep it light. Consider fresh fruit, not juice.

Desserts Anyone?

Generally, you should not spoil a healthy meal with a dessert. If however you are tempted, keep in mind the following:

Portion Control

Keep your serving portions of desserts, sweets, small. It only takes 30 to 60 seconds for a sugar craving to subside, so if you hang in there for long enough the craving will go. Recently, at a restaurant I was served a huge piece of cheese cake for dessert. It must have been packed with more than 1,000 calories. Was I going to eat that much only to give company to my dinner companion? Would it not be too high a cost to pay for friendship? I did the next best thing: I asked the waiter to pack up three quarters saying I would eat it later and ate a quarter. That quarter was 250 calories too many, but at least I had cut out on 750. Once I reached home, I placed the parcel in the fridge where it lay forgotten till thrown into the dustbin a few weeks later.

Eat Fruit

Fruit is good but not fruit salad as is commonly served. If you can avoid the sugary stuff altogether, it would be a great choice. A fruit salad can be quite misleading especially since it often comes laced with sugar syrup or a scoop or two of ice cream.

Drink Black Coffee

I use black coffee as a polite way to avoid keeping my dinner partner company with a dessert unless I really want it. They have the dessert they like and I have my black coffee. That way they are happy and I too end the meal on a 'lighter' note.

Things to do at home that will help you keep sugar at arm's length:

Clear Your Pantry

If you passionately want to rid yourself of the sugar menace, clear up your pantry of all processed and sugary foods.

Beware of Sauces

Sugar hides in most sauces. From the innocent-looking tomato sauce to the mustard topping that we love. They are all heavily loaded with sugar.

Look out for the sauce with less sugar or learn to eat without the condiment. The best way to bring this under control is to make your own sauces at home. The recipe is just a Google search away.

Shopping

When shopping, make it a point to look out for food items with the least added sugar. Do not go for the sugar-free alternatives, they are likely to be loaded with substitutes and fats.

Habits to be Controlled

There was a point of time when I would be mindful of my calorie intake during the day only to come home late at night and raid the fridge for a piece or two of chocolate. I was simply unable to control my craving for sugar. If you suffer from a similar malady, keep healthy alternatives at hand. I keep a bunch of fresh grapes at hand. When I eat couple of grapes (not too many), I am back in control. I ultimately got even wiser and smarter. I keep a strip of chewable vitamin C at hand. It is both sweetish and sour and it serves its purpose by giving me a healthy shot of the great vitamin instead of a sugary end to my day.

To sum it up, build a sense of awareness. Have what you want but *know* what you have. Do it by choice, not out of ignorance. The more the awareness, the better the choices and the better your health will be. Now, let me share my learnings with you.

Diets That Have Made a Big Difference in My Life

We have looked at the micro level at what we should not eat. Now let us have a look at what we should be eating—three main diets that have made a big difference in my life. I have also recommended a mix that I follow. You too should mix and match a combo that will keep you happy and healthy. This will be easy if you understand the concepts that form the basis of these diets.

I wish you first study them in detail and only then decide what you want to adapt or adopt.

The word diet has its roots in the Greek word diaita meaning a way of living.

The Mediterranean Diet: A Heart-healthy Diet[124]

The Mediterranean diet generally consists of the following basic components:

- Carbohydrates: 55 per cent (focus on low glycaemic index foods)
- Fats: 30 per cent
- Protein and fibre: 15 per cent

As one will understand from the very name of the diet it is set around the tastes, traditions and habits of the

---

124 Jessica Migala, Medically Reviewed by Lynn Grieger, 'What Is the Mediterranean Diet? A Detailed Beginner's Guide', Everyday Health, reviewed on 2 August 2022, accessed on 9 July 2023, https://www.everydayhealth.com/mediterranean-diet/guide

people living around the Mediterranean Sea. In this diet, meals are set around local plants and animals. There is high consumption of olive oil on salads and foods in this diet. In India, we could substitute olive oil with canola, sesame or even coconut oil depending on our tastes. So, while we discuss the typical Mediterranean diet, I suggest you look at it from your own local perspective. If you feel the diet is on the lines that you like, you could use foods available in your local area. There is nothing hard-wired.

Scholars have observed that this traditional diet which has a high level of carbs and a low level of fat as well as protein actually reduces the risk of heart disease and also assists in extending the lifespan of the people following it. Studies have proven that those following the Mediterranean diet are also less likely to suffer from cancer, Parkinson's and Alzheimer's.

In my opinion, this diet should be a favourite if you do not need to lose weight and are just on maintenance.

Chief Characteristics of a Mediterranean Diet

- A major portion of the meal consists of plant-based foods, wholegrains, legumes, vegetables and nuts.
- The preferred oil is olive oil. Should one want to do some deep frying or similar then canola oil, sesame oil or coconut oil is recommended.
- Herbs and spices substitute salt. Red meat, fish and poultry consumption is limited to twice or thrice a week.

- Generally, one would consume at least one glass of red wine with a meal.

Typically, breads are made of wholegrain and generally are low in unhealthy trans fats. Bread is an important constituent of the meal and is generally consumed by dipping in olive oil and not with butter.

Nuts form an important constituent of a Mediterranean meal. They bring in a lot of calories from their healthy fats which are not saturated. It is however recommended you keep the portions of nuts within limits due to their high calorific value. An important feature of the Mediterranean diet is that it does not limit one's consumption of fats but focuses on their quality. It nudges the dieter to choose healthier fats. The recipes are designed in such a way so as to discourage the consumers from using saturated and hydrogenated oils which contribute towards heart disease. Olive oil which is a monounsaturated fat is the chief 'fat supplier' of this diet. Research has shown that olive oil proactively reduces LDL cholesterol. Virgin and extra virgin olive oil also provide a lot of antioxidants to the meal.

A word of caution to us in India who eat a lot of fried food: olive oil has a very low flashpoint and so should not be used for frying. The oil used for frying or high-heat cooking oil generally is canola or others. This is high in monounsaturated fats and polyunsaturated fats and comes with the beneficial linoleic acid and omega-3 fatty acids which has a myriad of health benefits.

Mackerel, sardines, herring and salmon are all high in omega-3 fatty acid and are regularly consumed in this diet.

No Mediterranean meal is complete without a glass or two (or three) of red wine. The antioxidant benefits that are received from the wine are quite well known and combined with the low level of alcohol that it brings along serves to reduce the risk of heart disease quite a bit. However, if you are prone to excessive drinking, it would be wise to totally avoid wine.

The Mediterranean diet is not only about food, it is a way of living. In which conviviality plays a major role. These people usually eat their meals with family and friends and are quite a convivial type of society.

The Palaeo Diet[125]

If you ask me why, my answer is quite straightforward: we are Stone Age bodies living in a space age.

A multitude of well-controlled experimental studies have confirmed beyond a shadow of a doubt that low-glycaemic-load diets improve health and promote weight loss. The Palaeolithic (Palaeo) or Stone Age diet is one such diet. Similar high-protein diets are also known to be a very effective strategy in improving blood chemistry and helping with weight loss. The Palaeo diet is high in animal protein, omega-3 fats, monounsaturated fats, vitamins, minerals, phytochemicals and fibre, and low in

---

[125] Beth W. Orenstein, Medically Reviewed by Roxana Ehsani,'The Palaeo Diet: How It Works, What to Eat, and the Risks', Everyday Health, 30 December 2022, accessed on 9 July 2023, https://www.everydayhealth.com/diet-nutrition/the-Palaeo-diet.aspx

salt, refined sugars, cereals, dairy products, vegetable oils and processed foods.

During the Palaeolithic period, humans were hunter-gatherers. The food they consumed was what they could hunt, forage or fish. Obviously, food was fresh and not processed. The Palaeo diet tries to mimic or come as close as possible to the food groups that our hunter-gatherer ancestors lived on.

These Palaeolithic ancestors did not eat cereals (cultivated grains) or dairy products since they did not domesticate cows. Their diet was based on fresh fruits and vegetables, nuts and seeds, and meats and seafood. There was no consumption of processed food. Major studies point to the Palaeo diet as being a great one. Palaeo enthusiasts are often heard saying, 'Our genome has been based on this ancestral environment. We are Stone Age bodies living in the space age.' If you agree with this, you will understand why this diet can add a few years to our lives. If you are into weight loss, it also gives insights into why the hunter-gatherers were not obese.

In the Palaeolithic days, hunter-gatherers preferred meats to grass and within that they were known to prefer fatty meats to lean meat. So much so that if they killed a prey, they would first eat up the fatty part of the carcass like the marrow, the brain, the fat around the gut, the liver, the kidneys, and then, if still hungry, eat up the rest of it or else discard it. Going by these indicators, it is safe to say that the Palaeo diet was low in carbohydrates and high in protein. The Palaeo theory is that in a typical diet of an obese person carbs occupy approximately 53 per cent while in Palaeo diets, carbs would range from 25 to 35 per cent and the rest would consist of proteins and fat. The hunter-gatherers generally got all their carbs from fruits and vegetables.

There is a huge debate today that saturated fats are not too bad if eaten on their own. Theory has it that saturated fats become lethal when eaten with a high-carbohydrate food item. Some studies even show that if you eat bacon and eggs on their own, they are not bad but if you eat bacon, eggs and a doughnut, you are as good as poisoning yourself.

It is clear that given the availability of food for the hunter-gatherers they would never be able to have a diet where they got less than 10 per cent of their calories from saturated fats. The human genome has been conditioned by a high saturated fat intake, say Palaeo supporters. This could explain why there is lactose intolerance, acne problem and obesity.

Time-restricted Feeding[126]

'Humans live on one quarter of what they eat; on the other three quarters lives their doctor.' An inscription on an Egyptian Pyramid in BC3500.

---

[126] Jennifer Berry and Dylan Bailey, Medically reviewed by Grant Tinsley, 'Is Time-restricted Eating Effective for Weight Loss?', MedicalNewsToday, updated on 6 March 2023, accessed on 9 July 2023.

It is truly intriguing how ancient Egyptians had this thought. What it means is very simple. The lesser you eat, the healthier you become.

The Time-restricted Feeding (TRF) has a lot to do with circadian rhythms[127] and is based on the fact that all lives on this planet are born to a light and darkness cycle. The human being is a diurnal animal and has to wake up early in the morning to go out and search for its food. It has always been essential for us to have a clock which would tell us when to wake up and when to go out to catch our prey. The sun served as a good one. Similarly, most organs in our body are also known to have their own inbuilt clocks that tell them when to prepare for the arrival of food and when to take a break for repairs and maintenance. This timer readies our organs for peak performance and also keeps them informed when to lie back and rejuvenate.

In the years gone by scientists worked on the premise that each part of the brain had a certain function. While researching they found a 1 sq. cm area in the brain which they identified as the master clock of our body.

Studies by experts like Dr Satchidananda Panda[128]

---

127 'Circadian Rhythms', National Institute of General Medical Sciences, accessed on 9 July 2023, https://nigms.nih.gov/education/fact-sheets/Pages/circadian-rhythms.aspx

128 Emily N. C. Manoogian, Lisa S. Chow, Pam R. Taub, Blandine Laferrère, Satchidananda Panda, 'Time-restricted Eating for the Prevention and Management of Metabolic Diseases', Oxford Academic, Endocrine reviews, 22 September 2021, accessed on 9 July 2023, https://academic.oup.com/edrv/article/43/2/405/6371193

show that the median intake duration of food (the amount of time people spent eating) was 14.75 hours per day. Put plainly, if one starts with breakfast at 8 a.m. one would continue snacking or eating till about 10.45 p.m. Leaving only the sleeping time for our stomachs to get a break. Contrast this with the pre-1970s, when having three meals a day was the norm and one would start with breakfast at 8 a.m. and end with dinner anytime between 6 p.m. and 9 p.m., leaving an eating span of 10–13 hours but with much lower overall quantities. Dr Panda's studies proved that when those obese persons eating more than fourteen hours a days were simply asked to curtail their eating times to 10–11 hours a day, they lost an average of 7.2 pounds even though they were not asked to change what they ate. It is still debatable as to whether weight loss as a result of fasting or time-restricted eating is a result of time restriction or a reduction in the overall quantity of food consumed eating but a major reduction in obesity is easily obtained and the overall health benefits are humungous. Studies suggest that if one uses time-restricted eating in sync with one's circadian rhythm it works even better.[129]

In this case, I would recommend eating most of your meals during the day. Even insulin reacts differently depending upon whether food is ingested early or late at night.

---

[129] Marta Garaulet, Purificación Gómez-Abellán, 'Timing of Food Intake and Obesity: A Novel Association', ScienceDirect, 24 January 2014, accessed on 9 July 2023, https://www.sciencedirect.com/science/article/abs/pii/S0031938414000031

Here all patients ate the same amount of food with the only difference being that half ate between 8 a.m. and 8 p.m. while the others ate between 8 a.m. and 2 p.m. Both groups ate three meals and all the participants were pre-diabetics. The study found that mean insulin levels dropped significantly together with insulin resistance. A similar effect was seen in their blood pressure.

Just in case you think this system of eating will leave you feeling famished and distraught, I am happy to state that you are absolutely wrong. This does not leave your stomach growling and hurting for a refill. It is surprising that those who ate early felt satiated longer and hence could not eat more at night even if they wanted to. Somewhat counter-intuitively, restricting eating till 2 p.m. often resulted in more feelings of fullness that lasted through the night. While the original form of TRF from 8 a.m. to 2 p.m. is better since it keeps in sync with the cicadian rhythm, it is not easy to follow since most of us tend to have our main family meal at night. Do consult your doctor before embarking on.

The problem is only to start and be regular at it even though you do not want to be doing this every day of the week.The obesity goalposts have been changing so often starting with the time when we were guided to reduce fats in our meals to the time we were told to cut off sugars and to increase carbs to now where we are told that fats are not that bad after all. When possible however, you must eat healthy! TRF is also commonly called intermittent fasting and has generated a lot of interest due to its ease of implementation and visible results. One however has to be aware that even when practising TRF what you eat is important. So you must follow the basics especially regarding sugar. Never embark on this diet unless you have consulted your doctor.

My Diet Mix

Going through all the possible diets (many are just passing fads) can make one utterly confused. And making the right choice can be a difficult exercise because they all appear to be good. You could easily land into quite a mess if you followed a bad one unknowingly. It could be dangerous because the wrong diet could result in a damaged kidney or liver or both.

Weight loss alone should never be your sole target. It should always be good health. Weight loss will follow automatically.

There is a lot of statistical data that proves that those who follow diets high in animal foods do not live as long, get heart disease and even have a higher incidence of cancer. I therefore recommended the two diets we just discussed be mixed up which will help you become healthy. Before you start on any diet, I advise you to speak to your doctor and get some medical advice. You should try and minimize or totally eliminate simple carbohydrates from your diet. They do not have nutrient density in them. They carry almost no fibre but wreck your blood sugar.

Below is a list of the main troublemakers (simple carbohydrates) that you should absolutely avoid:

- Sugar in any form especially refined sugar. Be aware of sugar in fruit juices.
- White rice.
- White flour, pasta, bread and similar.
- Processed foods like bacon and ham.

I lost 5 kg in twenty days by following TRF.

Once you gain an understanding what healthy food is all about, you will realize that you do not need to be on any fixed diet plan but can eat whatever you want to and whenever. This is because by then you will be not only more food literate, but also more focused on your overall health. You will no longer feel like overeating too much and prioritize your health even if you go off course once in a while.

Ageing: An Enzyme to the Rescue

9

Meet Ming the Mollusc: The Oldest Documented Animal on Earth

In affluent countries, more than 85 per cent of the population will survive past the age of seventy-five, and the figure was only 20 per cent 150 years ago. Since in all these years barely a few managed to live beyond 120, experts believed that there was a limit to human longevity.

Animals display a bewildering variety of lifespans from mayflies that live for a few hours to the bowhead whales[130] and giant tortoise that live for more than 200

130 Laura Cross, '7 Animals With Incredibly Long Life Spans', vetSTREET,

years to even the koi fish[131] which was found to be more than 226 years old. Researchers have reported that Ming the Mollusc, a hardshell clam, is 507.[132] It holds the record for being the oldest documented animal on earth.

The jellyfish[133] and hydra[134] are supposed to have found a way of defeating death and may actually be immortal. The jury is still out on this. There are claims that the humble jellyfish never dies. If one looks beyond the animal kingdom into the plant world, the sequoia tree lives for more than 3,000 years and the bristlecone pines clear 5,000.[135]

---

29 June 2012 accessed on 19 July 2023, https://www.vetstreet.com/our-pet-experts/7-animals-with-incredibly-long-life-spans

131 Sean Perry, '5 Facts About Koi Fish' petMD by Chewy, 29 September 2022, accessed on 19 July 2023, https://www.petmd.com/fish/care/evr_fi_facts-about-koi-fish

132 Samantha Larson, 'Oldest Clam Consternation Overblown', National Geographic, 18 November 2013, accessed on 19 July 2023, https://www.nationalgeographic.com/animals/article/131116-oldest-clam-dead-ming-science-ocean-507

133 Emily Osterloff, 'Immortal Jellyfish: The Secret to Cheating Death', Natural History Museum, accessed on 19 July 2023, https://www.nhm.ac.uk/discover/immortal-jellyfish-secret-to-cheating-death.html

134 Emma Berthold, Expert review by Alistair G.B. Poore, 'Is it Possible to Escape the Slow and Steady Progression of Ageing?—The Animals that can Live Forever', Australian Academy of Science, accessed on 19 July 2023, https://www.science.org.au/curious/earth-environment/animals-can-live-forever

135 Craig Welch, 'What's the Oldest Tree on Earth—And Will It Survive Climate Change?' National Geographic, 31 May 2022,

The Hayflick Limit

In 1961, the renowned scientist Leonard Hayflick published a theory that came to be known as the Hayflick Limit.[136] Hayflick propounded that a normal human fetal cell population would divide between 40 and 60 times in a cell culture before gradually deteriorating.

Hayflick interpreted his discovery as an explanation of how ageing occurs at the cellular level. The ageing of cell populations appeared to correlate with the overall physical ageing of a human being.

Most of what we have experienced may tell us that Hayflick was right but with the information we now have I can tell you very authoritatively that if we work at it, we can have a long while to live, much longer than Hayflick imagined.

While discussing epigenetics, I have touched upon the DNA. In this chapter, we will look at DNA[137] from a slightly different angle. Your DNA contains your genetic code. Every time a cell divides, it has to copy that code but the new piece becomes shorter than the original one

---

accessed on 19 July 2023, https://www.nationalgeographic.com/environment/article/whats-the-oldest-tree-on-earth-and-will-it-survive-climate-change

136 Geoff Watts, 'Leonard Hayflick and the limits of ageing', The Lancet, 18 June 2011, accessed on 20 July 2023, https://www.thelancet.com/article/S0140-6736(11)60908-2/fullt

137 A Cleveland Clinic medical professional, 'DNA, Genes & Chromosomes', Cleveland Clinic, reviewed on 20 May 2022, accessed on 20 July 2023, https://my.clevelandclinic.org/health/body/23064-dna-genes--chromosomes

and every time the cell is divided the DNA also would get a bit shorter than it was before.

Why is this relevant? Because every time your body makes a copy of the DNA, the DNA would get shorter and after many copies, the genetic code in it would no longer be the same due to various errors that would creep in due to poor copying. Nature however being quite intelligent adds back a piece of DNA to its end as an extension. This extension is called telomere. Telomere attrition contributes to diabetes, cardiovascular disease, Alzheimer's and even cancer besides otherwise affecting our healthspan.[138] In this way, the genetic code does not get disturbed every time our cells divide since the telomere adds to the DNA length and a complete copy can be taken. However, every time a copy is made a bit of the telomere length is lost. As we age and we lose more telomere lengths, we reach a stage when the DNA starts getting exposed and cut. That is when the cells begin to signal to our brain that they are no longer required and are ready to die. According to Hayflick, after about 50 to 60 divisions we would run out of telomere.

This was truly a depressing situation, wasn't it? It meant that a maximum of 120 years was the limit of human longevity irrespective of what we did.

138 Hans-Jürgen Gruber, Maria Donatella Semeraro, Wilfried Renner, Markus Herrmann, 'Telomeres and Age-Related Diseases', National Library of Medicine, PubMed Central, 27 September 2021, accessed on 20 July 2023, https://www.ncbi.nlm.nih.gov/pmc/articles/PMC8533433

The Hayflick theory was sealed till Nobel laureate Dr Elizabeth Blackburn discovered that there existed an enzyme called telomerase,[139] which adds to the length of the telomere. If adequate telomerase was available, the telomeres would lengthen every time the cells divided. In this theory, our cells could have a relatively immortal lifespan. But it was subsequently discovered that supplements of telomerase caused cancer, so this idea had to be discouraged.

We now knew that telomerase was good for telomeres but supplements of it were bad, so the question was: What could we do to influence telomere length and the natural secretion of telomerase by our body?[140] To answer this, we need to understand what affects the secretion of telomerase.[141]

---

139 Brittney-Shea Herbert, 'The Impact of Telomeres And Telomerase in Cellular Biology And Medicine: It's Not the End of the Story', National Library of Medicine, PubMed Central, 24 January 2011, accessed on 20 July 2023, https://www.ncbi.nlm.nih.gov/pmc/articles/PMC3822486

140 Interview by Zoë Corbyn, 'Elizabeth Blackburn on the Telomere Effect: It's about Keeping Healthier for Longer', The Guardian, 29 January 2017, accessed on 20 July 2023, https://www.theguardian.com/science/2017/jan/29/telomere-effect-elizabeth-blackburn-nobel-prize-medicine-chromosomes

141 Jue Lina, Elissa Epelb, 'Stress and Telomere Shortening: Insights from Cellular Mechanisms', National Library of Medicine, PubMed central, HHS Public Access, 1 November 2021, accessed on 14 January 2024, https://www.ncbi.nlm.nih.gov/pmc/articles/PMC8920518/#:~:text=Stress%20induces%20secretion%20of%20glucocorticoids,to%20short%20and%20dysfunctional%20telomeres

- The feeling of a lack of love shuts off the telomerase production line. Self-love is most critical and is one of the biggest drivers of telomerase. So, learn to love yourself.
- Too much stress is a real killer and needs to be managed. You must manage stress.
- Gratitude is essential. A feeling of happiness at being alive keeps telling our cells that they need to produce telomerase to keep us living. If you do not like your life, the body shuts off the production of the enzyme.
- Being an altruistic person who is committed to an activity is one of the most effective stimulants to the body releasing a maximum of telomerase. When you have a mission to do something and when your nervous system commands your cells to stay healthy by saying, 'I am not ready to go because I have a job to complete that is very important'. Your body is stimulated to release telomerase.

Therefore, if you have a desire to do something good for this planet and its people and if you love your body, you will live healthier and longer.

What Does the Young-at-heart, Healthy And Happy Eighty-seven-year-old Paul Teach Us about Life

Below I have narrated the life of a senior citizen who lives a long, happy and healthy life. Where are you in this continuum? It is never too late. Give yourself a chance.

If you are not doing well, see what successful, healthy and happy people do and adjust your lifestyle to follow successful agers.

This is the story as told to me by a relative Peter, who a few years ago I had advised on how to keep his dad happy and healthy by giving him a reason to wake up every morning (His name is changed as he has requested confidentiality.) He is ever so grateful. For the sake of brevity I have picked up those parts of his story which will bring out the points I wish you to understand regarding increasing one's lifespan. The resultant story therefore appears very simplistic but the essence of it is absolutely true and may be emulated.

'My father Paul (name changed) is eighty-seven. He has outlived my mother who died about six years ago. He outlived all of his siblings and almost all of his relatives. His friends have become fewer and rarer since almost all of them had moved on to the lodge above. He lives in an apartment with a male nurse to assist him. I take care of his needs and arrange for his meals every day.'

Peter adds, 'Dad usually wakes up at around 5:30 or 6 in the morning. Does a bit of meditation, microwaves a hot cup of coffee and reads the local newspaper *The Navhind Times* which is regularly dropped at his doorstep by the local village boy. He then makes himself a light breakfast and sits down to read the paper from

> ***'Therefore, if you have a desire to do something good for this planet and its people and if you love your body, you will live healthier and longer.'***

cover to cover. If there is an interesting crossword puzzle it is a bonus. The whole 'affair of newspaper' takes him about two hours.

'He then exercises by lifting a few lightweights and does light knee bends and while holding on to his bed does a few sit-ups. He is now ready for his three times a week, 2-kilometre walk in the park within his building complex.

'He gets back home and takes a shower. By then it would be about 11:30 and his TV time. His favourite channels are the BBC and CNN and for news on India he turns on NDTV. When he is in a relaxed and happy mood he enjoys the serial *Two and a Half Men* and I love joining him to see it.

'Having had lunch he then walks away to his bed for siesta. Being well exercised he has a good nap and is in dreamland for about three quarters of an hour. In the evening, he is back to television and generally likes to watch programmes on Discovery Science. Once every fortnight he visits his doctor. Having known him for more than twenty years the doctor is quite a friend to him and spends about half an hour examining and conversing with him on his life and his achievements of yesteryears. On his way back, Paul looks forward to a rendezvous at the local store where he picks up a few of his favourite biscuits, a dark chocolate and a magazine to last him for a few days. During the week, he makes it a point to meet up with a few of his younger relatives and once in a while even invites them over for a drink and snacks. Having had a scotch, he can almost always be heard exclaiming, "What a wonderful world. Life is good!"

'He often invites his children and grandchildren out for dinner and is regularly invited by his kids for evening outings. Dad has fixed up Saturdays to spend time with us his kids. On Saturdays, he looks forward to either all of us or at least a few taking him out to dinner.

'Alone at home after dinner, he is on his iPad playing chess with virtual friends. While playing with virtual friends he is aware that no one either knows his age or who he is and so no one will either feel 'sorry' for him or give him a chance to win. He sets himself up for a good chess fight and has fun. He wins some and loses others but importantly he gets his adrenaline rush and goes to bed a happy and contented man after having a few pills.'

Now what makes Paul happy and contented?

- He has set for himself a routine he loves and goes about it almost every single day.
- From his statement, 'What a wonderful world. Life is good!' one infers he is happy with his life.
- It is obvious that he is not going to die lying down. He exercises and so keeps his tissues moving and muscles exerted. His morning walks give his lungs fresh air, get his heart pumping and his body all warmed up.
- He has not become a recluse but keeps himself abreast of the happenings in the world by catching up on news. This not only keeps his interest in life going, but also means that he does not have to keep talking about his 'good old days' all the time. This empowers him to engage in a decent

conversation on current affairs. He also watches comedies sitcom and science channels to keep himself entertained and informed.

- He goes out with his family often. This gives him the love and a sense of belonging, which is critical for a fulfilling life.
- He plays chess which keeps his adrenaline flowing.
- All that Paul is doing is working in his favour. I am sure his telomeres will be well conserved and growing. This will help him live a happy, healthy life for many, many years to come.

How to Eat Sensibly

10

Vegetables form a major source of our nutrients. However, all too often, we lose most nutrients because we do not know how to cook vegetables.

Tips for Cooking Vegetables the Right Way

Did you know that by cooking vegetables in as little water as possible, you could retain the maximum amount of vitamins and minerals?

I have tried to answer all your doubts in the following FAQs: [142]

---

[142] Franziska Spritzler, Medically reviewed by Atli Arnarson, 'How

1. *Which cooking method is the best to retain vitamins?* Steaming.

2. *How much of nutrients are lost while cooking?* Steaming and boiling may result in a loss of 25 to 35 per cent of vitamin C. Pressure-cooked vegetables retain more than 80 per cent of their vitamin C.

3. *How can I cook and optimize nutrient retention?*
   - Steam or blanch vegetables.
   - Stir-fry vegetables and meats.
   - Bake meats and fish but avoid baking vegetables.
   - Avoid boiling food in too much water.
   - Avoid reheating.

4. *Does roasting of vegetables result in major loss of nutrients?* Roasting, grilling and stir-frying are also pretty good ways of retaining nutrients and hence are recommended.

5. *Which is better? Steaming or roasting vegetables?* The answer would depend on the vegetable in question. Steaming is recommended for the more

---

Cooking Affects the Nutrient Content of Foods', 7 November 2019, accessed on 20 July 2023, https://www.healthline.com/nutrition/cooking-nutrient-content#cooking-amp-nutrients

sensitive veggies like broccoli but the general rule would be to keep the temperature, time and water to the minimum when cooking vegetables.

6. *Which are the foods that are recommended for steaming? What is the duration recommended?*
    - Spinach: 4 minutes.
    - Green peas: 4 minutes.
    - Broccoli, cauliflower, beans: 7 to 8 minutes.
    - Carrots, potatoes: 8 to 10 minutes.
    - Turnips: 15 to 20 minutes.
    - Kale: 12 minutes.

7. *Does vinegar act as a disinfectant even for E. coli?* Yes, vinegar is a great disinfectant and disinfects vegetables and fruits to the extent of about 98 per cent bacteria. Use one part white vinegar to three parts water to make a vinegar bath. Soak fruits and veggies for two minutes. Then rinse them in water.

8. *Is apple cider vinegar a good disinfectant too?* Yes, it is antiviral, anti-fungal, antibacterial and antiseptic.

9. *Is broccoli best eaten cooked or raw?* Recent research indicates that broccoli contributes more healthy nutrients when lightly cooked.

10. *How do you preserve maximum nutrient while preparing a meal?*
One can retain as much as possible of the vitamin and nutrient content of a meal by taking the following points into consideration:
    - Retain the skin of vegetables where possible.
    - Avoid reheating of food.
    - Use minimum water possible while cooking.
    - Use boiling as a last resort while keeping steaming as the first.
    - If the food is boiled, use the leftover liquid for soup in cooking.

11. *Is eating raw spinach and carrots healthier?*
Research has proven that cooked spinach and carrots are better. Cooked spinach and carrots come with high levels of beta-carotene, which is an antioxidant that has positive effects on the heart and is even known to protect against cancer.

12. *Which vegetables help weight loss?*
Leafy greens like spinach, kale cruciferous veggies like broccoli, cabbage and a few others are low in calories but high in fibre and minerals and therefore do help with weight loss.

13. *Can a banana be eaten daily?*
Eating excess fruits may trigger headaches and

sleepiness. The USDA recommends adults eat less than two cups of fruit a day. It recommends a maximum of two bananas a day.

The number of people who did not get infected by the Corona virus but have gone into depression because of the challenging environment is stunning. Mental illness is highly debilitating but often easily manageable. At the cost of repetition, I must remind you that your gut plays a critical role and can do a lot to help you live a healthy and long life. If you do not treat it with the respect it deserves, it is sure to throw many spanners in your way.

There is emerging evidence that the gut flora (that is, the microbiome) plays a key role in the regulation of our mood, cognition and anxiety. We are only beginning to discover the potential of food as a medicine. And the potential is mind-boggling.

It is pertinent to know that 90 per cent (the rest is produced in the brain) of our feel-good hormone serotonin is made in the digestive tract. Low levels of serotonin have been linked to irritable bowel syndrome and even osteoporosis.

'There is emerging evidence that the gut flora (that is, the microbiome) plays a key role in the regulation of our mood, cognition and anxiety.'

A study to understand which of the essential nutrients required by the human body were anti-depressant in nature was published in the *World Journal of Psychiatry*:[143]

[143] Laura R. LaChance, Drew Ramsey, 'Antidepressant Foods: An

The following are the anti-depressant nutrients:

- Folate
- Iron
- Long-chain omega-3 fatty acids
- Magnesium
- Potassium
- Selenium
- Thiamine
- Vitamin A
- Vitamin B6
- Vitamin B12
- Vitamin C
- Zinc

The foods that are rich in most of these nutrients are:[144]

- Oysters, mussels and various seafood
- Organ meats of animals
- Spinach, lettuce and other leafy greens
- Mustard and turnip
- Bell pepper
- Pumpkin

Evidence-based Nutrient Profiling System for Depression', National Library of Medicine, PubMed Central. World Journal of Psychiatry, 20 September 2018, accessed on 20 July 2023, https://www.ncbi.nlm.nih.gov/pmc/articles/PMC6147775

144 NHS Health Scotland, 'Vitamins and Minerals', NHS inform, updated 30 April 2020, accessed on 20 July 2023, https://www.nhsinform.scot/healthy-living/food-and-nutrition/eating-well/vitamins-and-minerals

- Cruciferous vegetables like broccoli and cauliflower
- Fresh herbs like cilantro, basil and parsley
- Wholewheat, blueberries and yogurt

How to Live a Healthy, Happy Long Life

Take Care of Your Brain

While every part of our body is important, our brain is probably the most important one. Unfortunately, most of us however do not know what is good or bad for its maintenance. I have compiled a few points which I am sure you will find interesting.

Ways to Support Your Brain?145

PHYSICALLY

- Supplements like gingo, jinsing, ashvaganda and thiamine are known to promote brain health.[146]
- Physical activity does wonders to the brain. Sports like badminton and table tennis are great.

---

145 Kerri-Ann Jennings, Medically reviewed by Kathy W. Warwick, '11 Best Foods to Boost Your Brain and Memory', Healthline, updated on 23 January 2023 accessed on 20 July 2023, https://www.healthline.com/nutrition/11-brain-foods

146 Kelsey Kunik, Medically reviewed by Jillian Kubala, Healthline, 'The 5 Best Brain-Boosting Supplements', updated on 7 September 2022, accessed on 20 July 2023,https://www.healthline.com/health/best-brain-boosting-products

When possible, dance your nights away. Dancing activates the cerebellum, which has a huge role to play in cognition.[147]

- Inflammatory foods like sugar is the biggest culprit.[148] If possible do away with it totally. Though it gives us a 'feel good' sensation, exercise does the same thing but with no inflammation. Keep your fasting blood sugar down, as high blood sugar promotes brain atrophy.
- Do not go on a fat-free diet as most fat-free food comes loaded with sugar. Also remember, 60 per cent of the weight of our brain is fat.[149] Wild salmon and avocado are foods for the brain.
- Obesity is a brain killer.[150]

---

147 Sharon Theimer, 'The Olympics for the Rest of Us: How Ping-Pong Can Help Your Brain', Mayo Clinic, 31 July 2012, accessed on 20 July 2023, https://newsnetwork.mayoclinic.org/discussion/the-olympics-for-the-rest-of-us-how-ping-pong-can-help-your-brain

148 Amy Reichelt, 'A Neuroscientist Explains What Sugar Really Does to Our Brains', Science Alert, 19 November 2019, accessed on 20 July 2023, https://www.sciencealert.com/research-shows-sugar-can-change-your-brain-here-s-how

149 Adrienne Santos-Longhurst, Medically reviewed by Seunggu Han, 'What Is the Physical Composition of the Human Brain?', Healthline, 8 April 2019, accessed on 20 July 2023, https://www.healthline.com/health/is-the-brain-a-muscle

150 Harvard Health Publishing, Harvard Medical School, 'Men's Health–Obesity: Unhealthy and Unmanly', 1 March 2011, accessed on 20 July 2023, https://www.health.harvard.edu/mens-health/obesity-unhealthy-and-unmanly

- Food has to be both delicious and nutritious. Ask yourself if you love the food laid in front of you and *if it loves you back*?
- Instead of sugar, get attached to the good foods that will love you back. Initially this will not be easy, but with practice and a little focus it will become natural.

Psychologically

Get rid of the things that infect and infest your mind. I am a serious pusher of positive thinking wherein we not only accept everything as they come, but also push for results while accepting failures as experiences or stepping stones. I believe in milestones as they suggest progress. You should proactively move on without getting stressed out or flustered. Here are a few suggestions on how you can add positivity to your life:[151]

Ask yourself if your behaviour or thinking supports a healthy brain. If the answer is no, change the way you think. Remind yourself that you desire to have a long and healthy life. Make it simple and keep it easy.

However bad yesterday may have been, it is over. Start every day on a happy note. Remind yourself that it

---

[151] Nasrin Shokrpour, Shima Sheidaie, Mehdi Amirkhani, Leila Bazrafkan, Ameneh Modreki, 'Effect of Positive Thinking Training on Stress, Anxiety, Depression, and Quality of Life among Hemodialysis Patients: A Randomized Controlled Clinical Trial', National Library of Medicine, PubMed Central, 30 June 2021, accessed on 20 July 2023, https://www.ncbi.nlm.nih.gov/pmc/articles/PMC8318152

has the potential of being a wonderful one. A lot depends on your thinking.

Flood your senses with happiness. Visualize images of Nature at its best. Feel the good sense of touch. Aromas of vanilla and jasmine go straight to your limbic brain and instantly give you a happy vibe, so keep these essential oils or fragrances at hand.

Socially

You may not realize it but your friends and extended family can play a major role in making you a happy and content person thereby keeping your mental faculties in good shape.[152]

Ask yourself what you have done during the course of the day to enhance your relationships. This may appear insignificant but it is critical to your longevity.

Purposeful people are happier and live longer. Take stock of what you have done during the day to be purposeful.

[152] Mayo Clinic Staff, 'Friendships: Enrich Your Life and Improve Your Health', Mayo Clinic, Healthy Lifestyle, Adult Health, 12 January 2022, accessed on 20 July 2023, https://www.mayoclinic.org/healthy-lifestyle/adult-health/in-depth/friendships/art-20044860

Increase Intake of Foods That Reduce Inflammation of the Body

Inflammation occurs when your body's chief defenders, the white blood cells, perceive an attack on your body and move to protect you from infection. If inflammation is not controlled, the body's immune system inflicts damage on itself. It is almost as simple as that. Our response should be to understand why this happens and then to give our body the nutrients and support that it needs so that it can control this effect. You could get into serious problems if your body remained chronically inflamed. Chronic inflammation has been linked to a host of diseases ranging from cancer. diabetes to even the dreaded Alzheimer's. A body's reaction resulting in inflammation is caused by various controllable and uncontrollable stressors like pollution, food sensitivities and allergies, obesity.

Food And Spices That Reduce Inflammation of the Body

There are many different herbs and spices that can reduce inflammation.[153] A few spices and herbs are listed below

[153] Camille Noe Pagán, reviewed by Neha Pathak, 'Spices and Herbs That Can Help You Stay Healthy', Compass by WebMD, Healthy Ageing Guide, 3 January 2019, accessed on 20 July 2023, https://www.webmd.com/healthy-ageing/features/spices-and-herbs-health-benefits#:~:text=%E2%80%9CHerbs%20and%20spices%20fight%20inflammation,which%20are%20healthful%20plant%20chemicals.%E2%80%9D

that will help you handle this situation. Focus on what is easily available to you.

Turmeric

Ayurveda has for centuries used it for its curative properties. It is a very potent anti-inflammatory agent. It also has great antioxidant properties.

Green Tea

The effects of green tea on keeping cardiovascular disease and cancer at bay are well established. Recent studies have confirmed that it also helps in the treatment of arthritis. Three to four cups of green tea daily is a healthy choice.

Chilli Peppers (Capsicum)

It is a great antioxidant. Capsicums fight free radicals, boost the immune system and have an anti-inflammatory effect on the body. Beta-carotene is used by the body to make vitamin A. This vitamin is crucial for good eyesight, bone strength and skin health among other things.

Black Pepper

This unassuming spice packs an anti-inflammatory punch. Its distinctive flavour has been shown to reduce inflammation.

Resveratrol

This is an antioxidant found in many plants. It is found in significant quantities in the skins of red grapes. It is a strong anti-inflammatory agent. Recent research indicates that it even protects against DNA damage and mutations.

Rosemary

Rosemary is a potent antioxidant and anti-inflammatory. It also assists digestion and enhances memory and concentration.

Cloves

Because of its anti-inflammatory effects in the mouth, the unassuming clove is a centuries-old home remedy for toothaches. Cloves and clove oil may be applied directly to the gums to help with a toothache.

Ginger

The anti-inflammatory effects of ginger help with osteoarthritis. Its main constituent gingerol has powerful medicinal properties which also help treat nausea and morning sickness in pregnant women, muscle pain and soreness. It even helps fight flu and common cold.

Cinnamon

In addition to being anti-inflammatory, cinnamon also comes with antioxidant, anti-diabetic, antimicrobial, anti-cancer and lipid-lowering properties. This miraculous spice comes from the bark of cinnamon trees native to China, India and South-East Asia. It even plays a role in fighting neurological disorders like Parkinson's and Alzheimer's.

Increase Intake of Antioxidants

Antioxidants play a vital role in our defence systems. Cells release micro waste matter into our body called free radicals. This happens while they process food and all else that cells get to process from our environment. Left to themselves, free radicals cause severe oxidative stress and are best neutralized lest over time they damage healthy cells thereby impeding the overall functioning of our body. Oxidative stress has been found to enhance the chances of heart disease, cancer, Parkinson's and a host of other deadly sicknesses.

Antioxidants[154] have donor atoms that go in search of free radicals to neutralize them. By taking care of free radicals, antioxidants boost our health. While there are

[154] Atli Arnarson, 'Antioxidants Explained in Simple Terms', Healthline, Nutrition,12 July 2023, accessed on 20 July 2023. https://www.healthline.com/nutrition/antioxidants-explained

many antioxidants, the two main ones that I recommend you to focus on are glutathione and vitamin C.

Glutathione[155] is probably the most important antioxidant needed to stay healthy and prevent ageing, cancer, heart disease and dementia. Many claim that it is even good at preventing the dreaded Alzheimer's. The good news is that our body produces its own glutathione. However, being super-sensitive it quickly gets depleted when attacked by pollution and the toxins we ingest through a poor diet. Stress and infections too play havoc with glutathione. A very low level of glutathione in our body leaves us exposed to the ravages of oxidative stress which is easily supported by free radicals that see it as an opportunity for them to pull us down. Our toxic levels even hamper the recycling of glutathione. That puts us into even deeper trouble. Fortunately, there are ways to augment this antioxidant by consuming vegetables and fruits rich in sulphur like onions, garlic and the cruciferous family of broccoli, kale, cabbage and cauliflower. Exercise is also a great way to increase it.

Generally, antioxidants are found in fruits and vegetables, they come in the form of beta-carotene, vitamin C and vitamin E.

---

155 Nazzareno Ballatori, Suzanne M. Krance, Sylvia Notenboom, Shujie Shi, Kim Tieu, Christine L. Hammond, 'Glutathione Dysregulation and the Etiology and Progression of Human Diseases', National Library of Medicine, PubMed Central, 2 October 2009, accessed on 20 July 2023, https://www.ncbi.nlm.nih.gov/pmc/articles/PMC2756154

Nuts also are a great source of antioxidants. Walnuts come on top but almonds, pistachios, hazelnuts, cashewnuts and macadamias are also high in antioxidants. While papaya, banana and orange are well known for their antioxidant content, cranberries, blueberries and blackberries are known to carry the highest antioxidants among fruits. Your daily brew of coffee and tea are rich in antioxidants too.

Research has shown that too much of antioxidant supplements could cause harm, and increase the risk of cancer.

Increase Intake of Fibre

We cannot complete a discussion on food without discussing fibre. It is Nature's favourite nutrient.

Human nutrition is no plaything. It is extremely complex but the choice we have is clear. Either we continue looking at food as entertainment and end up eating what in the long run makes us sick or we treat it with respect knowing that it brings with it essential supplies required by our cells to manage the more than 100,000 chemical reactions taking place in our body almost every second. A chronic shortage of even one essential nutrient could affect the chemistry of our entire body and with time result in diseases.

Fibre[156] is an unassuming but important part of our

---

156 'The Nutrition Source', Harvard, T.H. Chan, School of Public Health, last reviewed April 2022, accessed on 20 July 2023, https://www.hsph.harvard.edu/nutritionsource/carbohydrates/fiber

diet. It is technically a carbohydrate and comes in two forms—soluble and insoluble. Soluble fibre dissolves in water and often forms gels which are digested by gut bacteria. This is found in oats, apples and beans. Soluble fibre is especially good for heart health. It is associated with decreased risk of cardiovascular disease and lowering LDL.

The average human being needs roughly 30 grams of fibre per day. We most often end up with less than ten. Depending on the study you look at, we are either eating 30 per cent of the quantity we need or 40 per cent of our requirement.

Fibre keeps us feeling full longer. This is because digestion is delayed keeping us feeling satiated longer which even helps with weight control. It also enhances insulin sensitivity.

Let us compare what happens when we eat two different breakfasts. A bagel topped up with jam will get through your digestive tract in no time. The 300-calorie breakfast will soon be over and in no time leave you feeling hungry all over again.

Compare this to a wholewheat bagel with a high-fibre peanut butter for breakfast. Just like the bagel with jam, this one would also have 300 calories but take much more time to digest and so would leave you feeling full for longer. The same is true for foods like white rice. The fibre content of white rice is negligible. Much like sponge, soluble fibre soaks up the bad cholesterol and pushes it out in the stools. Fibre even helps reduce your liver's production of cholesterol.

A good example of insoluble fibre is cellulose found in broccoli and celery. Legumes, nuts, wholegrains, fruits and non-starchy vegetables (cabbage, cauliflower, eggplant) are also great sources of dietary fibre.

When we eat, the excess energy generated is deposited as glycogen in the liver and the rest as triglycerides in fat tissue. When we fast or are hungry, energy from the liver and fat is withdrawn from these stores. It is difficult to understand why when we are designed with this wonderful system, we should still be eating every few hours. It is like having a Ferrari in your fleet of cars but never using it.

Our[157] ancestors hardly ever had obesity issues and almost never suffered from cardiovascular disease or diabetes even during their times of plenty. That too after living on a diet where they got a lot of their calories from meats! The same was true for societies like the Kitavans[158] and Okinawans[159] that ate mainly carbohydrate-rich diets.

---

157 Susan Gallagher, 'What Can Hunter-Gatherers Teach Us about Staying Healthy?', Duke Global Health Institute, 21 April 2019, accessed on 20 July 2023, https://globalhealth.duke.edu/news/what-can-hunter-gatherers-teach-us-about-staying-healthy

158 Staffan Lindeberg, Erik Berntorp, Peter Nilsson-Ehle, Andreas Terent, Bengt Vessby, 'Age Relations of Cardiovascular Risk Factors in a Traditional Melanesian Society: the Kitava Study',ScienceDirect, accessed on 20 July 2023, https://pdf.sciencedirectassets.com/782868

159 David Robson, 'A High-carb Diet May Explain Why Okinawans Live So Long', BBC, 100 Year Life, accessed on 20 July 2023, https://www.bbc.com/future/article/20190116-a-high-carb-diet-may-explain-why-okinawans-live-so-long

Things changed for man about ten thousand years ago with agriculture.[160] It was at this stage, man started farming which reduced his need to hunt for food. As food was easily available, it probably started the 2–3 times meals a day.

Looked at from this angle, quite a few of our diet-related problems may not necessarily be only about carbs and proteins but could just as well be because we eat too often.

160 Erin Blakemore, 'What Was the Neolithic Revolution?', National Geographic, 5 April 2019, accessed on 20 July 2023, https://www.nationalgeographic.com/culture/article/neolithic-agricultural-revolution

How Mental Spring-cleaning Can Help You

11

We have discussed a lot about our physical being. What we most often forget is our mental health, which plays a decisive role in how we think, feel, receive stimuli and respond to all that life throws our way. It not only affects our ability to cope and overcome stress, but also build relationships and recover from setbacks. Whether it is to cope with a specific health problem, to handle emotions better, to feel more energetic or to simply feel happy and satisfied, this chapter will give you a road map to follow.

What Does Good Mental Health Look Like?

Being mentally healthy has a lot to do with our

psychological well-being. It is a lot about how we feel about ourselves, the depth of our relationships and our ability to manage our feelings and responses in times of adversity and stress. Positive thinking is important but we cannot be perpetually free of at least some amount of anxiety, stress and even sadness. To have a happy and fulfilled life despite trials, adversity and even misfortune is what this chapter is all about. Good mental health does not imply only an absence of mental sickness. You should do a fact check on yourself. Take a look at yourself and find out how mentally balanced you are. Mentally healthy people generally possess the following attributes even in times of adversity. Undertake the following exercise and if you do not measure up too well consider ways by which you could bolster your situation.

- *They are latently content people* who enjoy life. Are you like this?
- *It is easy to make them laugh* since they keep their sense of humour intact irrespective of situations. What about your sense of humour? Do you laugh often?
- *They are people with high self-esteem* who may have failed in the past, have come back from the brink and have confidence in their ability to do it again. Have you ever failed at something you yearned for? Are you a confident person?
- *They have a reason to wake up in the morning* and look forward to the next day. What is your reason to wake up in the morning?

- *They are happy to learn new skills* when required and are not embarrassed to learn from their juniors. Are your skills adequate given the changing world scenario? If you need reskilling are you ready or embarrassed?
- *They do not overdo anything* and live a balanced life which is a mix of work, play and relaxation. Where do you stand in this equation? Do you spare time for yourself?
- *They get into meaningful relationships* which take time to build but remain intact through trials and misfortune. How do you rate your relationships? Do they need improvement?

Look at yourself objectively and decide how many of these characteristics do you have. If not, make a special effort and cultivate a few. It is not difficult if you do it consistently. Over a period of time, it will become a part of your personality.

Tips to Boost Your Mental Health

- Take good care of your gut.
- Keep yourself physically fit.
- Use auto-suggestion or visualization to bolster your self-image.
- Get sound and adequate sleep.
- Manage stress. Do not let it get to you.
- Be grateful for small and big graces.
- Where possible, practise letting go.

- Having good friends is a long-term asset. Make friends and keep them.

Just like the physically healthy people, mentally healthy ones are more likely to quickly bounce back from illness or injury; mentally healthy people are better equipped to cope with stress, adversity and even misfortune. They remain focused and adaptive during both good times and bad. These people live by the philosophy that every problem has a solution and go in search of the key to open every closed door. When they are put down, they bounce back quickly. Studies have shown that during the recent pandemic most of the fatal victims did not have the attributes of the mentally healthy people I have discussed about above.

In our modern world, it is quite common for people to suffer poor mental health. Almost one in five persons suffer from some mental condition or the other. Unfortunately, very few seek help and remain stuck in a rut only because they do not recognize that they have a problem or they are embarrassed to see a counsellor. They try covering up their condition expecting it to go away on its own. However, just like so many untreated physical ailments it most often does not disappear and causes long-term avoidable mental and even physical damage.

The good news is that one need not seek medical help always. One of the primary culprits that trouble our mental peace is stress and we must learn to manage it. The biology of ageing has been studied from time immemorial. However, only in the last fifty years or so it is becoming increasingly clear that stress greatly facilitates ageing. Stress could be the difference between ageing quickly and ageing gracefully. It could be the difference between our biological age and the chronological one. It could be the reason why a thirty-year-old looks like a fifty-year-old and a sixty-year-old looks like a forty-year-old.

Elissa Epel, PhD, a professor of psychology who is the co-director of the University of California, San Francisco (UCSF), Metabolism and Emotions Center says, 'The biology of ageing and the biology of stress are intimate friends, and they talk to each other and influence each other. The greater the feelings of chronic stress, the greater the signs of ageing in cells.'

Chronic stress often leads to a build-up of pro-inflammatory factors called cytokines which mobilize our immune system to release chemicals meant for the defence of our body to turnaround and attack the very cells they are meant to defend. Chronic stress is even known to impair mitochondria, the energy centres of our cells, which in turn further promotes ageing.

Tips to Reduce Stress

Fortunately, there are changes we can make to reduce stress in our lives as well as to reverse the cell damage caused by it. It is not even difficult to manage stress. All it takes is to make small changes in the way we view life. Small tweaks over a period of time, go a long way in keeping our biological ageing at a slower pace than the chronological one.

Research has shown and it is also quite obvious to anyone who cares to notice that when most of us get stressed we do the exact opposite of what we are supposed to do. When stressed, we tend to sleep less, drink more alcohol and exercise less. Smokers smoke more, while introverts get into a shell and sometimes totally withdraw from social supports as a result getting even more stressed out. We then get disillusioned with life and neglect ourselves resulting in falling sick.

It is important to understand the cause of stress before responding to it. As you face a stressor, it is important to solve the problem by figuratively rolling up your sleeves and doing away with the stressor. For example, if you have an impending exam you study and focus on ways to pass it. Your response to a stressor should not be emotion- focused because in this case you are doing nothing to change the stressor but it is doing something about how you feel. So keep your response practical, not emotional.

Now imagine that you have studied for the same exam but you are still feeling very anxious. There are various ways to overcome your anxiety like talking to friends, watching a movie or indulging in a hobby. Basically, doing anything that takes your mind away from the stressor and keeps it in a more positive state; this will reduce the impact stress can have on you.

A lot of life can be cyclical
I feel better when I do better
I do better when I feel better

The pointers below will help you understand how to manage stress. At no stage should you feel that stress management is only about thinking positive and hoping for the best. This approach is utopian and at worst can be quite catastrophic. It is more about people who live by the philosophy that every problem has a solution and go in search of the key to open every closed door. When they are put down, they bounce back quickly.

Our feelings guide our thoughts which affect our behaviours. These three are interrelated and if one is changed the others also change in order to be in equilibrium. For example, if you are feeling sad, your behaviour will reflect that and so your thoughts will be negative and in turn will only serve to enhance your feelings of sadness and loneliness. You could alter the cycle by going out with friends or chatting with your loved one or doing something that you love. This will result in your thoughts changing and then you would end up in a better mood.

Following are a few ways in which you can handle stress:

- *Ask yourself how likely is this stressor to occur again?* A lot of the time we get stressed out because we overestimate the likelihood of the event causing the stress to reoccur.
- *Recollect if you have worried too much about a similar situation earlier?* It is important to ask yourself this question because it is common to exaggerate the negative impact of an occurrence.

- *Ask yourself what are the likely outcomes if what is stressing you actually happens*? Try not to think of multiple worst case scenarios because this type of thinking can freeze your mind leaving you incapable of taking the right decisions. Instead, think objectively keeping in mind the chances of the stressful events reoccurring.
- *Ask yourself, how long the situation that is causing you stress will last*? Should things go wrong will the effects be long term or will they be manageable and forgotten in a month's time? As a thumb rule, if you are unlikely to remember the incident after three years have passed, you should not fret too much over it.
- *Do not be harsh on yourself even if you have failed in the past*. You could use your failures as a learning experience and avoid committing the mistakes.
- *What are the best and worst case scenarios*? The answer to this question could give you a lot of solace and confidence.
- *Get your mind to think of possible out-of-the-box solutions to the problem*. Could you learn more about the stressor or could you find someone who could help you understand it better? Take the help of friends and well-wishers with whom you can discuss your problem. A different perspective always helps.

Ask yourself the following questions:

- What do I need to cope with this stressor?
- Which of these resources do I have at my disposal?
- What new resource(s) do I need to acquire to deal with the stressor?
- Have I underestimated my ability to cope in the past?
- Whom can I contact in my social circle to help resolve the situation?

Keeping a diary can be quite cathartic.

It is common that when we take up a new job or an assignment the first few months can be quite stressful. And many feel ill-equipped and blame themselves for not being smart enough, or wondering about how their new colleagues feel about them.

This type of a feeling is not only bad, but also unfair. Left unchecked it could breed on itself and make things terrible. If you have started a new job, you need to give yourself some time to adapt to the new situation. You may also need time to gain the required skills and knowledge to perform in your new job. Should you not handle yourself well, you could end up quitting and get even more depressed.

Here is an exercise that will help you adjust your feelings especially when you are feeling down.

- Name one thing that pleasantly surprised you today.
- Name one thing that positively moved you.
- Describe one thing that inspired you.

These questions should help you think of the good times you have enjoyed and get your happy hormones moving again. We often forget the positive things we have achieved while clinging on to the negatives.

Your opinion of the world may change if you change your world view. Instead of seeing life from prisms that cause you stress, look at life through eyes filled with gratitude. Find things in your life to be grateful for. You need to be mindful of your present rather than dwelling in the past especially if it has not been too good.

Social service is another important pillar protecting us from stress. Hence, caregivers who have a greater number of positive emotional connections appear to be protected from much of the damage caused by stress. In addition, meditation, exercise and an anti-inflammatory diet can reduce help reverse some effects of ageing. From my years of experience and research, I believe bio-hacks like weight loss pills that promise weight loss without exercise and diet control or protein powder diets that similarly promise a great body with no effort most of the time are amazing elixirs but come with unforeseen side effects that often leave us much worse than before. Making small incremental lifestyle changes will over the years go a long way in keeping our cells healthy and happy.

Norman Vincent Peal so aptly put it when he said that there was only one place on earth where a person can have no stress at all and that was in their grave. Stress is an inevitable by-product of modern life.

Hence, I have always advocated stress management and not stress avoidance.

Your Daily Routine to Manage Stress

Work on yourself so that you are in a better position to manage stress. Take baby steps at first but with time you will have to pick up the pace. Put into your daily routine the suggestions given below.

Activity Scheduling

- Use your calendar to record your average daily moods.
- Schedule at least two fun activities to do in a week.
- Have a well-balanced diet of activities that will give you a sense of mastery and a sense of achievement. It could be something as simple as cleaning your closet.

Get into a State of Relaxation

Practise meditation. It will help you relax but do not make it goal-oriented because that will have the opposite effect. There will be times when you will have better meditation session and others when you will end up feeling the session was a bad one. This is normal and to be expected.

Exercise

Exercise is a great way of getting into a good mood. It is quite underrated as a stress buster.

Connect with People

Meaningful relationships (including those with pets) that are not necessarily romantic are the most consistent marker for a good quality of life and a key ingredient in coping with stress. Strong family and social bonding can be of great help.

Prayer

Prayer gives you a connection with something bigger than what you are and works as a great support.

Have a Purposeful Existence

He who has a 'why' to live for can live with any 'how'. Know your 'why' and make it meaningful to you. If you do not have one, find it but make your life meaningful to its last breath. For many people, the 'why' could be family. This in many ways explain why after children have grown up and left the nest parents tend to age quickly. It is because their reason to live is no more. The secret to living is to always find a new 'why' when the old one is no longer relevant.

Maintain Healthy Relationships

Having a healthy relationship with your inner circle of close family members and friends can go a long way in keeping you stress free.

Create a Social Support System

Refer to the following diagram. Right at the centre of the circles is *you*. List out from closest to furthest whom you can depend on and for what. You will have someone you can depend on for problem solving, but they will be absolutely useless if emotional support is required. The same can be true for those you consider good at emotional support. By doing this exercise, you will have a ready reckoner to be used when you feel overwhelmed.

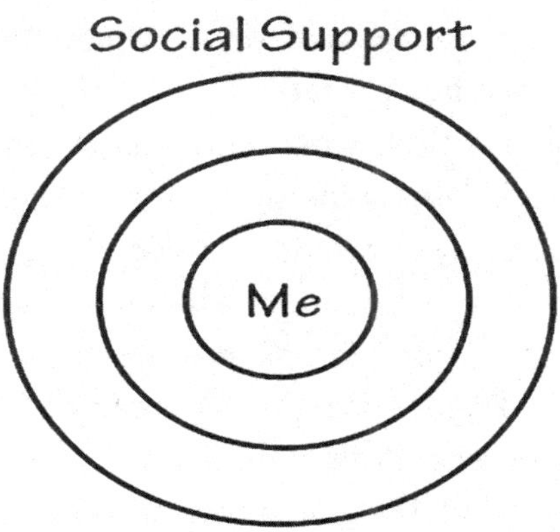

Thus, once you understand that stress cannot be avoided but can be managed, you will start finding ways to manage it. Know that within limits stress is good and needed. Good stress, or eustress, is the type of stress you feel when you are excited. Your pulse quickens and your hormones surge, but there is no threat or fear. You might feel this type of stress when you ride a roller coaster, compete in a game or go on a first date.

Benefits of Nurturing Close Friendships

Let us not forget that we are both physical and spiritual beings. Friendships affect our spirit the most. If we are physically perfect but mentally and spiritually broken, it will not help us a bit. It will soon start reflecting on us physically. We need to be happy in all facets of our lives. It is not just about having a good friend who will comfort you when in trouble or will take care of you when you are sick; it is much more. In the Blue Zone regions, people do not compartmentalize their lives. Their physical and social worlds mingle together and work to complement each other rather than being apart.

I remember a time when I was all stressed out by a problem at work. I knew the solution to it was at hand but just could not apply my mind to solve it. I just needed to calm my mind so that I could refocus. Just then a close friend of mine, Ernest, knocked at my door and walked in. That was all I needed to get my head off the problem. A cup of coffee and a few minutes with him was just the break that I needed. I resolved the matter as soon as I got back to the problem with a clear mind.

All this was possible because of what was going on in my body at a chemical level. At the time before Ernest appeared, anxiety was causing cortisol to course through my body and started to put me into a panic mode thus paralysing my mind. In a nutshell, I could no longer think logically. When Ernest walked into my office, serotonin was released by my body and the release of cortisol stopped therein allowing my mind to get back to normal.

That is how I could solve my problem with a cool mind after Ernest left. Too much exposure to cortisol increases the tendency to suffer from chronic diseases like asthma, irritable bowel syndrome and arthritis. Have you heard of the phrase 'You can worry yourself to death?' It is not just a saying. If cortisol rules our bodies for too long, that is exactly what happens.

While having a close friend or two is the best, social groups also serve as emotional pillows and leaning posts which can come in handy. Studies have shown that cancer patients assigned to support groups did much better and had longer lives than those with similar problems that did not want to be assigned to any support group. There is certainly something life-giving in the exchange of empathy or sympathy between two people who may be traversing a similar path in life.

I have friends who have moved into isolation and prefer to be alone. While this may not be bad if they prefer solitude, in the long run a situation like this tends to make the person look inwards and away from society. This is when they move from solitude and fortitude to isolation. Humans are social animals and so it is inhuman to live in isolation for too long. We all crave company and when we do not get it, it takes a toll on our body. A part of us begins to die and we then start getting mentally disturbed by little things which set us off on to a trajectory of sickness and sadness which could easily spin us into a downward spiral.

Relationships are often not straight and clean. Sometimes they can even become messy and depressing, and hurt us badly. At times like these, the tendency is to get into a shell and we may seek isolation for solace. As long as we believe in the human race and know that it brings along with it the good, the bad and the ugly we should assume that having seen the bad now is the turn for a good friend to appear. The law of averages will catch up and we will find good people who exist to give us help and to be helped. They do exist, I assure you.

While being surrounded by friends is good and indeed important, you need to select the people you will be surrounded by. You cannot choose your family but you can choose your friends. You should also decide how much time you will share with each of them.

One of the secrets of my success is that I deliberately surround myself with positive-thinking and forward-looking friends. I shun negative people. It would however be utopian to expect a positive-thinking person to be optimistic.

The philosophy 'you can judge a person's character by the company he or she keeps' is a very profound truth that is often overlooked. Watch the people you hang around with. If they have an unhealthy lifestyle, it is likely to rub off on you. The saying, obesity is contagious, is true. It is much easier to live a pleasure-based sedentary life than to pursue health and wellness.

In a nut shell, friends bring you a lot which translates into good health in the long run.

- They improve your self-confidence and self-worth.

- They help you cope with traumas, serious illness, job loss or even the death of a loved one.
- They encourage you to change or avoid unhealthy lifestyle habits, such as excessive drinking or a lack of exercise. As a personal example, I owe a lot to my friend Guitry Velho who nudged me to start taking care of my health and got me to the gym.

Whatever be the case considering the comfort and enjoyment that friendship can provide, it is a worthwhile investment to nurture new relationships.

How Exercise Benefits Mental Health

There is yet one more important adjunct you need to look at which will help you both physically and mentally. That is physical exercise though it benefits our body only till a point. Beyond that, the benefits reduce drastically and at a point the wear and tear of our body begins.

'Achieving success is a challenge but so is struggling, you may as well choose success.' Rob Liano, bestselling author and motivational speaker

You must modify your exercise plan routinely because if you do not you will soon see diminishing returns. Be regular with your workouts, time your workouts, do not focus too much on machines, try circuit training and having a partner to exercise with could be fun.

There is a lot of research that has proven that interval training is an excellent way to burn calories. Interval training is nothing but workouts in which you alternate periods of high-intensity exercise with long low-intensity recovery periods. This builds up fitness and burns more calories. You must remember, though, that interval training is tough, so get into this after about a month of a simple exercise routine.

This will not only boost your metabolism, but also keep you relatively injury free. Do not make this weight loss challenge an inhuman one. Try to have fun while losing weight. As I said earlier, the choice is yours. It is important that you enjoy doing what you are. Do not only focus on weightlifting. There are huge health benefits to be reaped from doing cardio exercises too.

The Impact of Visualization on Mental Health

Auto-suggestion makes transformation easy though there are many misconceptions about it. The truth is that visualization, as auto-suggestion is often called, is a big tool and if used well one can banish negativity by superimposing all that is positive. You must learn and put visualization into practice and if you master this art you will not only improve your health, but also save a lot of money.

If you want things to get easier, you must reinforce positive ideas through repetition and perseverance much like prayers recited in various religions where one repeats a mantra or prayer for 10–50 times at a go. Repetition holds the key.

Visualization[161] is nothing but seeing through your mind's eye and feeling with your heart, body and soul what you wish to be.

This is not a system I have invented. It has been tried and tested for centuries. Advertisers use it all the time. Haven't you seen TV commercials projecting a handsome young man driving his family in a beautiful car? The advertisement is continuously repeated so that with time one feels as if one's car is not good enough and desires to buy a new one. This is nothing but visualization.

Perkins's tractors established the existence of the placebo effect clearly indicating that there exists within us a power that heals. Unfortunately, somewhere many years ago we lost our body's user manual and no one knows where to find the switch to turn on this healing power. Auto-suggestion could be the answer. It has the capacity to activate the self-healing process from within. When done in conjunction with medicine (if required) it could provide astonishing results. Studies have shown that when a medicine is taken expecting a quick recovery, the recovery is much faster than when the same medicine is consumed with no hope. Positive thinking does activate the healing power within. To enjoy good health you need to constantly see the good in life and stay positive. When you fall sick (which all of us do at some time or the other), it is imperative to plant a seed

---

161 Napoleon Hill, *Think and Grow Rich*, Random House UK, 2004.

of positive thoughts of healing and good health in your mind because these thoughts in turn send a message to the cells in your body that there is life to live for and that they should get into repair mode quickly. People who worry about a sickness they do not have, worry so much, that their body takes it as an instruction to develop the sickness. As a result, with time they actually suffer from it. It is very simple, have healthy thoughts and more often than not your body will match your thoughts and stay well.

Below are a few positive affirmations for good health. Use them as often as you possibly can. Repeat them at least thirty times a day for sixty days before they actually get deeply embedded into your psyche.

- I stay healthy because I eat healthy.
- I enjoy exercising.
- I thank God for a healthy body.
- Having perfect health is my divine right. God has given it to me and I am grateful.
- Every cell in my body is active and radiates good health.
- My body's defence systems are good and vibrant. They actively defend me against onslaught of any disease.

For auto-suggestion to be more effective, identify what it is that you want. Decide what is holding you back. Determine the obstacles you need to overcome. Figure out what you would like to substitute the obstacles with.

Chose to substitute whatever you want and then imagine it in your mind's eye.

To activate auto-suggestion, it is imperative that you spice up your thoughts with emotion and feelings. The more feelings are there, the better the results will be.

Auto-suggestion works best when you are positive. Hence, create a positive frame of mind. Avoid negativity at all costs. Use 'I am rich' instead of 'I am not poor' or use 'I am brave' instead of 'I am not scared'. Instead of 'I am not sick' use 'I am healthy'.

For auto-suggestion to take root and grow, repetition is imperative. The more you repeat with emotion, the quicker it will deliver to you the results you seek.

You are the David you sculpt. You are the Mona Lisa you paint. There is no one else who can do it for you. It is you all the way.

All these practices put together will equip you to handle the stress that comes your way but only perseverance and constant repetition will give you the results you will be proud of.

How Insomnia Is Detrimental to Mental Health

Sleep is very much underrated but it is a time for repairs and renovation.[162]

---

162 Joshua E. Brinkman,Vamsi Reddy, Sandeep Sharma, 'Physiology of Sleep', National Library of Medicine, StatPearls (Internet), last update 3 April 2023, accessed on 21 July 2023, https://www.ncbi.nlm.nih.gov/books/NBK482512

'You are the David you sculpt. You are the Mona Lisa you paint. There is no one else who can do it for you. It is you all the way.'

Sleeplessness contributes to depression, chronic fatigue and even obesity. The need to sleep is universal. Being sleep deprived for many days can be a killer. Even though the mechanisms of sleep are not yet fully understood, a lot of studies have shown that adequate sleep has a lot of positive effects on our body and helps restore our nervous, muscular, hormonal, skeletal and immune systems. Sleep helps us file away memories[163] so as to easily retrieve them when needed. If you are having trouble sleeping, you are not alone but among at least 30 per cent people with the similar problem. Unfortunately, it is common to treat the problem by consuming medicines prescribed by well-meaning doctors. The paradox here is that these tablets if consumed over a long period of time cause abnormal sleep patterns[164] and worsen the problem rather than solve it. More than 50 per cent of insomnia is because of stress, anxiety and a host of other issues.[165] Instead of addressing these causes, tablets treat

---

163 Björn Rasch, Jan Born, 'About Sleep's Role in Memory', National Library of Medicine, PubMed Central, April 2013, accessed on 21 July 2023, https://www.ncbi.nlm.nih.gov/pmc/articles/PMC3768102

164 Mayo Clinic Staff, 'Prescription Sleeping Pills: What's Right for You?', Mayo Clinic, accessed on 21 July 2023, https://www.mayoclinic.org/diseases-conditions/insomnia/in-depth/sleeping-pills/art-20043959

165 Krista Soriano,' Lack of Sleep Messes with Your Mental Health: 5

the symptoms. Since the cause has not been treated, the pills have to continue thereby making one dependent on them while also welcoming all negative side effects that the medicine brings with it.[166]

Many experts advise that healthy sleeping should be planned through the day rather than at night, but most people do not plan this until bedtime by when it is already too late. Our habits like what we eat and the time of dinner along with our intake of alcohol and caffeine have the potential of contributing to insomnia.

The best way to manage insomnia is to consume foods rich in tryptophan like eggs, tofu, cheese, milk and even pineapple.[167] Tryptophan is a building block for serotonin and melatonin which are hormones that also promote calmness of the mind, happiness and sleep. Other sleep-friendly nutrients include calcium, which strengthens and calms the nervous system and vitamin C which is essential for the production of serotonin. Regular exercise helps the body release stress and has also been shown to help

---

Signs You're Not Getting Enough', Psycom, updated on 8 June 2021, accessed on 21 July 2023, https://www.psycom.net/can-insomnia-cause-mental-illness

166 Andrew Gross, 'More than One-in-Five Fatal Crashes Involve Drowsy Drivers', Newsroom, AAA Public Relations, 11 March 2014, accessed on 21 July 3023, https://newsroom.aaa.com/2014/11/one-five-fatal-crashes-involve-drowsy-drivers

167 Edie Horstman, 'Not Sleeping Well? A Nutritionist Says These 10 Foods High in Tryptophan Could Be Sleep's Secret Weapon', Camille Styles, accessed on 21 July 2023, https://camillestyles.com/wellness/foods-high-in-tryptophan

sleep patterns. However, exercising just before bedtime could disturb sleep. Easy to implement and quick to help remedies like aromatherapy, sleep masks, dark curtains to block out light from getting into bedrooms, light instrumental music to calm the mind and cooling the room go a long way in getting a good night's sleep.

There is still a lot of research going on into sleep and what it does for us exactly.

Not getting adequate sleep can impact your mental health in ways that affect your day-to-day life. Do not take it for granted because the damage is real. Sleep deprivation[168] adversely affects your ability to make decisions and even to manage emotions. At times you have to manage stress, grief, fear and anxiety all at the same time. Without a good night's sleep, this becomes even more difficult since your cognitive ability gets impaired.

If a lack of sleep becomes chronic, you could suffer from acute depression and panic attacks.

A simple unassuming afternoon nap for twenty minutes has the power to influence your overall well-being and productivity. Short naps can actually be a powerful and highly effective way to cushion for an inadequate night's sleep. Research at the Johns Hopkins Sleep Disorders Center shows that the best time for siesta is between 1 p.m. and 4 p.m. Ideally, the nap should be for 20–40 minutes

---

168 Camille Peri, medically reviewed by Neha Pathak, 'What Lack of Sleep Does to Your Mind', WebMD, Healthy Sleep Guide, 7 June 2021, accessed on 21 July 2023, https://www.webmd.com/sleep-disorders/features/emotions-cognitive

and not more to avoid feeling too groggy immediately after waking. Longer naps may cause problems in falling asleep at night. Taking power naps for less than ninety minutes have been found to have a better word recall and by inference better memory compared to people who did not nap at all or napped for more than ninety minutes.

Longer naps however could cause a few unexpected problems.[169]

Dr Charlene Gamaldo advised that afternoon naps need to be limited if you are having problems with insomnia or taking more than thirty minutes to fall asleep at bedtime. You will need to keep yourself active and happy after your nap so that your night's sleep is not disturbed. A study has shown that adults may benefit from sleeping on a hammock.

If you take care of all the factors that boost mental health, you should be able to handle anxiety, depression, stress and practically all that life throws at us in a positive spirit. If after having made persistent efforts you still are not functioning at your optimal effectiveness at work, in your relationships or at home, you definitely should seek professional help.

Beyond sleep the following are great ways to pamper your mind, body and spirit, and thereby giving yourself the required support to overcome the various challenges.

169 Heidi Godman, 'Are You Napping Too Much?', Harvard Health Publishing, Harvard Medical School, 1 April 2023, accessed on 21 July 2023, https://www.health.harvard.edu/staying-healthy/are-you-napping-too-much

Massage as a Powerful Tool to Better Health

A massage is a powerful tool that not only helps you relax, but also helps your body get detoxified.[170] It is not a luxury. It contributes to general wellness in more ways than one and as a result has become very popular. Massages are no longer limited to luxury spas and upscale health clubs but are offered as therapies at clinics, hospitals, airports and at even not so high-end spas and health clubs.

A good massage eliminates tension in muscles and increases flexibility.

Kneading and working on muscles get fluids moving within the muscle and also pushes toxins out of the muscles[171] and into the kidneys for purification. It is for this reason that it is recommended that you drink water both before and after the massage. The kneading process also relaxes muscle tissue, releases compressed nerves and increases joint space while decreasing joint friction and stress. Relaxing tensed and painful back muscles can easily rid you of shoulder pain.

The most overlooked benefit of a massage is its ability to get toxins out of your body through the lymphatic system.

---

170 Patricia Lavers, 'Can Lymphatic Massage Really Help You Detox?', The Clara Clinic, accessed on 21 July 2023, https://theclaraclinic.com/blog-home/can-lymphatic-massage-really-help-you-detox

171 Ibid.

While more research is needed to confirm the specific and direct benefits of massage many studies have found that a massage is also helpful in so many other ways.

Anxiety Relief

- Digestive disorders
- Insomnia related to stress
- Sports injuries
- Keeping arteries healthy
- Post-operative care and recovery

Ordinarily a massage should leave you feeling happy and agile but feeling sore after one is quite normal for many. Some could even feel a bit fatigued. All will settle down in a matter of a day and there is no need to panic. This reaction by the body to a massage is called therapeutic inflammation. Since a massage releases free radicals and toxins from the knotted muscles, one may sometimes feel a bit sick but rest assured the immune system, kidneys and liver will take care of this situation and one will soon be back to normal and feeling better.

While a few forms of massage due to their very nature may leave you feeling a bit sore, the trick to avoid too much soreness is to ensure that the pressure being exerted on you is not too much or making you uncomfortable. Most massage-related problems arise due to excess pressure.

Without a doubt, it is probably one of the best stress busters ever known to man. Make it at least a once-in-a-month commitment to be kept.

Benefits of Taking Sauna

Besides massage another way to nurture your mind, body and spirit is by taking sauna.

If all I needed to do to maintain perfect health was to sit in a sauna,[172] I would do it every day of my life. I truly enjoy taking a sauna. If you have not tried one, you should.

Saunas were popular even in ancient times. [173]

Sauna provides better sleep, a relaxed mind and the sweating is an important way to naturally rid us of toxins.

Have you ever wondered why we have fever? This is because when we fall sick, our body gets hotter by raising its metabolic activity thereby killing pathogens and extricating toxins. Sauna too heats our body and we get a similar cleansing effect without actually falling sick.

Sauna also results in marginal weight loss, relieves sore muscles and joint pains, improves blood circulation and in the long run is also said to improve blood pressure. A sauna is super relaxing. You will at least come out of it feeling happy and energized.

Issues to Consider While Using Sauna

---

[172] MaryAnn De Pietro, Medically reviewed by Yamini Ranchod, 'What are the Benefits and Risks of a Sauna?', MedicalNewsToday, updated on 27 June 2023, accessed on 21 July 2023, https://www.medicalnewstoday.com/articles/313109

[173] Minna L. Hannuksela, Samer Ellahham, 'Benefits and Risks of Sauna Bathing', Science Direct, 1 February 2001, accessed on 21 July 2023, https://www.sciencedirect.com/science/article/abs/pii/S0002934300006719

Spending too much time in a sauna can result in dehydration. It is dangerous to be in a sauna under the influence of alcohol or drugs.

Do consult a physician before getting into sauna. Stay hydrated all the time. Drink up a glass of water and wet your face and head before entering the sauna. You could carry with you a bottle of drinking water.

After you are done, give your heated body some time to cool and return to normal. Spend about ten minutes relaxing on an easy chair and hydrate yourself.

Saunas are perfectly safe for most people as long as they stick to a maximum stay of twenty-five minutes, keep temperatures within the range I have suggested and stay hydrated both before and after the session.

What I have described above is the 'dry sauna'. You could also use the steam bath which is a 'wet sauna'.

Know Your Spiritual DNA

12

'In order to be happy we must first possess inner contentment; and inner contentment doesn't come from having all we want; but rather from wanting and appreciating; being grateful for all we have.' The Dalai Lama

Having dealt with body and mind, it is time for us to look into how we can use our spirit to further solidify our physical being to enhance our quality of life, immunity and even our longevity.

Our spiritual DNA is perfect . We have it all within us but with years of programming we have been brainwashed into believing in our weaknesses rather than in our strengths which have been hidden away from us.

How to Practise Gratitude

We only have to delve into our spiritual resources to understand how we are connected and power-filled. If you get this connection right, I guarantee you that you will add a few quality years to your life. One of the simplest resources that you can pull out of your bag is gratitude.[174]

As it turns out, gratitude has an array of benefits both for the one who is grateful as well as its recipient. A regular expression of gratitude is known to have positive physical and psychological effects. The special psychological advantages derived from gratitude combined with the benevolent act of forgiveness leaves one feeling joyous, contented and optimistic even resulting in a good night's sleep.

Studies have shown that the expression of gratitude releases 'happy hormones' which can even boost your immune system. So whether it is for the sake of being happy, fighting sickness or for longevity of life you must find ways of expressing gratitude. It is simple to be grateful. For some people, gratitude comes easily; for others, it can be a bit difficult. With time, however, it can be formed into a habit. A few ways are listed below by which you can cultivate the habit of being grateful for things big and small:

174 Amanda Logan, 'Can Expressing Gratitude Improve Your Mental, Physical Health?', Mayo Clinic Health System, 6 December 2022, accessed on 22 July 2023, https://www.mayoclinichealthsystem.org/hometown-health/speaking-of-health/can-expressing-gratitude-improve-health

- *Write thank-you notes* to friends and well-wishers to express gratitude for something they may have done for you. Write to yourself once in a while too. Self-praise is important too, especially in our modern world where gratitude is not always forthcoming.

'*Our spiritual DNA is perfect.*'

- *A gratitude journal can come in handy*. Write down on a daily basis the help and assistance you may have received. Also, add to your journal any gifts or tokens of appreciation that someone may have showered on you.
- *Think of all the good things that have happened to you* during the past few years. Vividly recollect the moments of celebration including the settings and sensations, of that given moment. The more vividly you get into the moment, the more meaningful your gratitude will be.
- *Be grateful for the 'taken for granted things'* like the sun that gives us light and warmth, the green grass and the bright stars on a moonlit night. These would make great themes for a sterling meditation.
- *Be grateful for the food* laid before you.

Being grateful seems very simplistic, but if you take the time out to read and research on the benefits of this unassuming attribute you will be astonished.

How to *Let Go*

Besides gratitude, another life support may be obtained by getting rid of the old and welcoming the new. This was so aptly put together by Buddha who is believed to have said, 'The secret of health for both mind and body is not to mourn for the past, worry about the future, or anticipate troubles, but to live in the present moment wisely and earnestly.'

One of Buddha's paramount teachings given more than 2,500 years ago was on letting go. Letting go[175] is easy if we learn it. The flip side is also true. Life can become very difficult if we do not understand how it works. Buddha tells us that all human struggles stem from attachment. While this thought may sound very simplistic, it is deeply profound. Take a hand-held mirror and dispassionately look into your life. You may be startled to see how true this is even for you.

How to Break Free

Arguments start from an attachment to our perceptions. We fail to see that there are two sides to the same coin only because we believe that the only existing side is the one we perceive. Arguments end up in anger if the

---

175 Mike Brooks, 'Hold On Loosely: Why Attachment Is a Double-Edged Sword', Psychology Today, 1 March 2022, accessed on 22 July 2023, https://www.psychologytoday.com/us/blog/tech-happy-life/202203/hold-loosely-why-attachment-is-double-edged-sword

result is not as expected. This is why many a time one ends shouting or talking aloud when in an argument. It is only because we are clinging to our positions scared that we may lose. The sadness we experience when we lose or fail to achieve what we set out to get is also the result of our attachment to the expected end result. We are comfortable with the status quo and prefer the security of clinging to it versus the turbulence of having to connect to an unknown anchor because change can sometimes bring along with it a tremendous amount of stress.

Having understood a little bit about how attachment takes its toll, you must understand that the accumulated ill effects cannot be noticed overnight. They creep on us with stealth.

Let us look at this thing we call attachment in more detail. Only once we scrutinize it and see it for what it is, it will be easier for us to let go of it. We believe that attachment to family or relatives, near or dear ones, lovers or just friends, begins gaining root after spending a lot of time with them but in reality we do not get attached to people. We get attached to the experiences we have with them. Two persons get connected due to an emotional connect. Our minds associate the emotions with the person and unknown to us we then crave more of the person primarily to get that pleasurable response. When we arrive at this place, we develop an attachment to the person and then start getting anxious about losing them. What we actually fear the most is missing out on the emotions this person exchanges with us.

The solution to this 'fear of loss' is to detach yourself and break free. This may sound inhuman, insensitive and uncaring but it is not any of this. It is not as frightening as it sounds. Have you never heard someone comment about a good friend, 'He is no longer the same person I knew'? That is only because that friend was ready to detach from you but you were not quite ready. Dependence on others feels good only when the conditions are favourable to us. When the conditions change, we get despondent. The truth is that we never find true happiness searching for it outside ourselves. Often detachment makes the person we have been attached to get more relaxed and comfortable as they feel less pressured to fit into the image we may have created of them. They then start loving us in ways that we least expect. This has often resulted in two extreme reactions: true love or extreme disgust! But it surely gives clarity to those involved. The easiest way to detach from others is to look for love within. In no way am I telling you to get selfish and only love yourself. When Jesus said, 'Thou shalt love thy neighbour as thyself,' he meant exactly that. First love yourself and only then will you be able to love your neighbour just the way you love yourself. If your cup of love is empty, you will have nothing to share with others. Fill your cup so that you can share.

Once your cup overflows, you will become less attached to people and even to material things. You will have the power to appreciate what you have without craving for it. You will love without conditions and not have to manipulate. Instead of worrying about losing the love you share, you will learn to enjoy the moment always knowing that it is bound to pass.

Understanding the doctrine 'this too will pass' will enable you to realize the impermanence of life. Contemplate this for a while and you will be exposed to the wisdom of not being attached to any person or thing. You will then stop fighting transience knowing fully well that life is transient.

Life is a journey and not a destination. Postponing happiness into the future is wrong because you should enjoy the journey. The problem starts when we attach our happiness to the end result of our future actions. If you think you will be super happy when you lose 5 kg in weight or when you get a raise at work, you need to bring yourself to the present reality and appreciate what *is* rather than what *can be* or *will be*.

Clinging to old wounds even after knowing that they will fester can have disastrous consequences. Peter whom I have coached did not forgive his teacher for more than two decades. I am sure his teacher would not even remember why! He clung to the memory of how his teacher told his mother that he was just average and lucky to be in her class. Till that moment, Peter was sure that he was brilliant but did not get great marks only because he was not diligent. He was stunned, shocked, embarrassed and hurt by his teacher. How could she misjudge him and go ahead and make such a pronouncement? That too to his darling and most revered mother? With Peter's pride smudged for life how could he forgive his teacher? He held on to the grudge for more than twenty years until I showed him how to let go. Letting go of the deep-seated wounds opens up our life to welcome new experiences that help us grow.

Regrets of what could have been and thinking of how our life could have been better are totally avoidable. As we progress, many things do not work out exactly as we had planned. It does not mean that we are to be blamed for the unforeseen or changed circumstance. Sometimes investments made with due diligence go bad and even though it may have not been your fault, you blame yourself for letting things go out of hand. You cling to what you have 'lost' as a result of the loss. The cars you could have bought, the villas that could have been yours or the missed club membership. Unless these thoughts are set free, they continue to spoil your today. A psychologist walked around the classroom teaching an interested batch of students. As she raised a half-filled glass of water, everyone expected they would be asked the oft-asked 'Half empty or half full' question. Instead, with a smile on her face, she enquired, 'How heavy is this glass of water?'

Answers called out ranged from 100 gm to 220 gm.

She replied, 'The absolute weight doesn't matter. It depends on how long I hold it. If I hold it for a minute, it's not a problem. If I hold it for an hour, I'll have an ache in my arm. If I hold it for a day, my arm will feel numb and paralysed. In each case, the weight of the glass doesn't change, but the longer I hold on to it, the heavier it feels.'

She was discussing this in the context of letting go and of how we should let go of thoughts that trouble us for long.

Learning to let go of things that do not bring you happiness will free both your resources and time for those who need you and those whom you want. It will make you feel light and bring tons of happiness into your life.

Put the glass down.

How Yoga Brings You Inner Peace

Can yoga add a few years to your life?

Yoga is the practice of what is called Hatha Yoga which stresses more on physical postures or asanas.

It is believed that yoga can serve as a complementary intervention[176] for cancer,[177] asthma and even heart disease. However, the jury on this is still out on this. I use yoga as a routine for physical exercise and mental relaxation. I strongly recommend that you do too. Yoga is not too complicated and hardly needs any equipment.

Yoga Makes You Ten Times More Flexible

During a yoga session one works multiple muscle groups at

---

[176] Arndt Büssing, Andreas Michalsen, Satbir S. Khalsa, Shirley Telles and Karen J. Sherman, 'Effects of Yoga on Mental and Physical Health: A Short Summary of Reviews', National Library of Medicine, PubMed Central, 13 September 2012 https://www.ncbi.nlm.nih.gov/pmc/articles/PMC3447533

[177] Ram P. Agarwal, Adi Maroko-Afek, 'Yoga into Cancer Care: A Review of the Evidence-based Research', accessed on 22 July 2023, https://www.ncbi.nlm.nih.gov/pmc/articles/PMC5769195

the same time. It includes stretches, folds and also bends which even move previously unfelt and unknown muscles.

Yoga Gives You a Good Posture

Most of us sit all day at a desk, then in a car and then in front of the television. Invariably, we end up with a hunch or at the least with a bad posture. Yoga has asanas that help straighten the spinal muscles, which in turn straighten your back and give you a good posture.

Yoga Is a Stress Buster

We are all routinely under some stress or the other. It is an integral part of our lives. Through the use of breathing exercises, yoga can help you take control of your mind thereby limiting the effects of high stress.

Yoga Is Good for Your Heart

Yoga is not a woo-woo exercise of psyching oneself. It goes far beyond that. Studies have shown that people who practise yoga routinely have much lower blood pressure than others.

Yoga Is a Powerful Tool against Insomnia

A good yoga workout followed by some relaxing asanas like, the shavasana will make you feel totally relaxed and even has the potential to put you to sleep.

Yoga Improves Gut Health

As we all know, an underperforming gut can precipitate various sicknesses. Yoga exercises take special care to strengthen the gut region. Yoga's body twists help give the gut just those many stretches that help digestion and bowel movement.

Yoga Is a Weight Loss Agent

Even though it is not promoted as an important weight loss agent, yoga does promote weight loss and builds up strength.

If you are a sceptic, you may think all the above is hocus-pocus and not for you. I practise all I have mentioned and assure you that at best you will be wrong and your life will be transformed and at worst you will feel good for having tried. Spirituality is a very personal experience, and everyone's spiritual path is unique. Research shows, however, that spiritual stress relief strategies as described above have been helpful to many, regardless of faith. Make time to explore spirituality.

Whether you are rediscovering a forgotten spiritual path, reinforcing your commitment to an already well-established one or wanting to learn more about spirituality, there are countless ways to start exploring your spiritual side and help improve your well-being.

My Experiments with Life

13

My Journey So Far

Having discussed various ways of enhancing the quality and longevity of life let me now share with you even more about how I go about my own life.

Do remember that it is not a 'one size fits all'. Each of us is unique, so you will have to figure out what works for you. You may need to consult a doctor before you start implementing the ideas I have shared.

Despite fasting being recommended through the ages, I was quite petrified of the very word fast. Starvation was a potent punishment in the days of old and fasting brought to mind vivid images of starvation, famine and drought. Hardly did I know that fasting and starvation were poles apart. And with time, I realized that starvation and fasting were like chalk and cheese. The former being disastrous, while the later life-giving. I now use fasting as a pivot for all that I do even though ultimately it is a combination of nutrition, fasting, autophagy, exercise, stress management, spirituality and socializing that makes me what I am.

I start my longer fasts at least thirty-six hours after a heavy workout. This is because the day after a heavy day at the gym I feel extremely famished and need to eat. My body needs to repair itself. By dinner the subsequent day, I am sufficiently nourished and rested and ready to be on a fast. Depending on my work schedule, I vary the schedule of my workouts and fasts. My intermittent fasts are generally from 8 p.m. to 2 p.m. the next day. There is nothing too great about this as all I do is miss breakfast. But it is not as easy as it looks since I have to be careful not to eat anything at all during the fasting period. Of course there are some who say that you could have butter in coffee or even bone broth, but for my 16-or 20-hour fasts I consume only water, black coffee or green tea without sugar or milk.

Fasting is not difficult if you try it. Importantly, it gives you a sense of being in control of your life in ways you would have never felt possible. These are all life-extending and life-ameliorating processes. Fasting is an important leg of what I call the tripod of my maintenance—nutrition, exercise and fasting.

In any case, should you want to formulate your own diet, I caution you not to follow a fad diet. When deciding what is good for you, keep sustainability in mind. Generally, diets too low in fat (unless that is what you like) are not sustainable in the long run. Research shows that our bodies yearn for fat and cannot stay without it for too long. Remember your brain is made up of a huge portion of fat. If you need to lose weight in the short run, no-fat diets would help for sure but you are likely to put it all back.

The paramount goal of many diets is to either get down to a desired weight or to maintain one's weight. In choosing the diet and the consequent lifestyle adaptations, try to get your spouse, family member, friend or well-wisher to do it with you. Support helps in a big way.

There is no magic bullet. All components of a diet make the whole weight loss programme.

I am a non-vegetarian. I love my food and am happy to eat almost anything that moves. Having studied various diets and with the idea of extending my beautiful life to the maximum, I have made a deliberate effort to increase my intake of veggies. I get most of my carbohydrates from vegetables and fruits. At least 50 per cent of my plate is made up of vegetables. Typically, I have meats for three meals a week and fish for at least two.

Having supplements is like delivering the groceries to a kitchen. Just as without groceries a chef cannot deliver good food, without supplements our body cannot give us its best. The best diet will go bad without adequate supplements. I do not split hairs about number of grams to be had as I believe that there is no need for such precision. Do not overdose yourself. If you do a good job of looking after yourself, you must reward yourself. The reward system for me is the spa. I visit a spa for a full body massage which I try to keep to twice a month. And sauna is a bonus.

I have worked at reducing toxins where possible. Be it in the number of creams I use which I have reduced or soaps. It just tells you that I have become conscious of what happens to my body when it is exposed to the chemicals that make up most lotions and soaps and so I have reduced my exposures.

Nothing would be complete if I only took care of my body. I make it a point to remind myself that I am a part of the whole universe. I make it a point to regularly connect with the universe within me and the one outside as well. Meditation forms a regular part of my life. I spend anywhere from 15 minutes to 1 hour almost every day meditating. I prefer doing it early in the morning. I meditate so much that sometimes when getting sleep is difficult, I have developed the ability to meditate my way into a deep slumber.

I regularly meditate on

- Gratitude
- Letting go
- The miracle I call my body
- The interconnected reality of the universe

I strongly recommend meditation. It is a fantastic way to achieve happiness and longevity.

Keep yourself engaged with finding your life's purpose and build structures around it so that you are positively and purposefully engaged. We often think we will be happy if we keep ourselves occupied all day. Being busy all day is okay for a while, but if you are to go a long way and remain happy and healthy you will have to busy yourself by getting involved in something that will give you a sense of purpose.

Get out of your comfort zone. Our brain, even though different, is much like a muscle and needs exercise. Keep it alert. No point having a healthy body and a sluggish brain.

Take risks. Not the 'make it or break it' risks but do take risks and expect to win but be prepared to lose. You cannot win all the time. Wage your bets astutely. The adrenaline push that you get from taking risks is important for your good health and longevity.

Did you know that by 2050, one in six people in the world will be over the age of sixty-five[178] and 426 million will be eighty or older. Not everyone will be able, fit and wanting to live on but I hope most will. There are already more elderly people on this planet than ever before. We need to step back and reflect. You need to have a plan since life is a marathon. Don't believe in age, believe in energy and do not let your age dictate what you do. If

[178] United Nations, Department of Economic and Social Affairs, Population Division (2019). 'World Population Ageing 2019: Highlights', (ST/ESA/SER.A/430), https://www.un.org/en/development/desa/population/publications/pdf/ageing/WorldPopulationAgeing2019-Highlights.pdf

you work at it and are lucky, your life will be a happy and fulfilling marathon. You must learn to pace it.

So, how do we go about planning for this marathon? Regrettably, we plan our finances but not our lives beyond a point and then get ourselves intc one big mess as we allow all our support systems to crumble without anything to lean on. The reality is whatever your age, if you do not plan in some detail for retirement you will be in a serious mess.

The Chemistry of Happiness

The chemistry of happiness is about the play of four main hormones in our body.

Endorphins

When we exercise, our body releases endorphins. This hormone interacts with receptors in our brains to trigger a happy feeling. Thus, exercising makes us happier. Laughter is another good way of generating endorphins. Spend at least thirty minutes a day exercising or reading funny articles or watching something funny on TV to get your daily dose of endorphins.

Dopamine

Along life's journey we pile up many little and big achievements. As we cross the finish line of each little or big accomplishment, our body releases the happy hormone dopamine. When we get appreciated for a successful task, we feel good because our body releases this feel-good hormone. This is why we get happy when we buy a new house, a new car, get a good haircut or a new shirt or a promotion. Dopamine is our friend. Go ahead and give yourself a pat on the back when needed. Self-praise is better than no praise especially when others do not recognize the good you do. Feel free to pat yourself on the back. You need the dopamine.

Serotonin

This hormone is released when we act altruistically. Do something which will help others. When we transcend ourselves and give back to Nature or to society our body gets happy and releases serotonin. Volunteering, making big or small social contributions, comforting an unwell friend get our body to release serotonin. Low levels of this chemical have been associated with depression. That is what makes volunteering so important.

Oxytocin

It is often called the 'cuddle hormone' or the 'love hormone'. It is released when we become close to other human beings. When we hug or kiss our dear ones oxytocin is released.

Conclusion

In a nutshell, exercise or laugh daily and get your thrill of endorphins, set yourself little goals to achieve and claim your dopamine, be good to the world and be assured of serotonin and finally live happily by hugging and holding your loved ones to get your shot of oxytocin. When we are happy, we become well equipped to deal with all life's challenges and adversities.

Happiness is a choice. If you want to be happy, you must stay healthy.

A Road Map to Longevity makes you the master of your life. While making you aware that life is not only about accumulating wealth, but also a lot about being physically and mentally well so as to be able to enjoy it. In the long run, no amount of wealth can make a sick man happy.

Rome was not built in a day, so do not expect results overnight. A healthy, happy and long life will be possible only if you start laying its foundations beginning today.

Eat your food as your medicine. If not, you may have to eat your medicine as your food.

If you want to walk fast, walk alone but if you want to walk a long life, walk together.

The following best doctors in the world are free and always at hand:

- Sunlight
- Rest
- Exercise
- Healthy and tasty food

- Self-confidence
- Friends

The road to your destiny is very long. Life is always a work in progress. Expect change and be happy to adapt to it. Without change, life would be boring and not worth the journey.

'Eat your food as your medicine. If not, you may have to eat your medicine as your food.'

Acknowledgements

My gratitude to my darling wife, Jean, and two adorable daughters, Charlene and Sheona, for their support and inspiration especially when things did not go the way planned.

This book would not have been possible if I had not read the findings based on research done by Dr Napoleon Hill; Dr Dale Bredesen; Raymond Francis; Dr Gary Taubes; Dr Loren Cordain; Dr Bodo Melnik; Dr Vanessa McMains; Dr Ray Shepherds; Dr Elisabetta Barbi; Dr De Magalhaes and team; Dr Brian Clement; Dr Robert H. Lusting; Dr Yoshinori Ohsumi; Dr Elizabeth Blackburn; Dr Robert McCarrison; Dr Bruce Lipton; Dr Stephen Anton; Dr Emmanuelle Passegué; Theodore

Ho Bob Proctor; Peggy Mccoll; Jeff Norris; Francesco Lagona; Nicola Davis; Nicholas Weiler; The John Hopkins University; The Cleveland Clinic; Harvard University; The Mayo Clinic; University of California, San Francisco; University of California, Berkley; The University of Roma Tre; The James Lind Library; World Health Organization; The University of Pennsylvania; The Guardian; Journal of the History of Medicine and Allied Sciences; University of Rochester; The World Journal of Psychiatry; Horizons in Bioscience and the University of Florida.

My gratitude to Ajay Mago, my dynamic and visionary publisher for publishing this book, to Chief Editor Shantanu Ray Chaudhuri for seeing merit in my manuscript and to Senior Editor Jyotsna Mehta for editing my manuscript with vision, enormous skill and precision. None of this would have been possible if not for my literary agent Dipti Patel who steadfastly stood by me and introduced me to Om Books International.